THE ART AND SCIENCE OF CRAFTING A COUNTRY'S IMAGE

THE ESSENTIAL TOOLKIT FOR TRANSFORMING NATIONAL IDENTITY INTO GLOBAL INFLUENCE

THIRD EDITION

CARMELO CUTULI

The Art and Science of Crafting a Country's Image:
The Essential Toolkit for Transforming National Identity into Global Influence
Third Edition
By Carmelo Cutuli
ISBN: 9798265230751
Copyright © 2015, 2019, 2026 by Carmelo Cutuli, *TWS*
First Edition 2015

CONTENTS

PREFACE

Throughout history, a nation's influence was measured by the size of its armies, the reach of its fleets, and the extent of its territorial borders. Power was tangible, geographic, coercive. Today the terms have changed. In an era of information abundance and attention scarcity, the old metrics of national power no longer hold. The currency of modern statecraft is not only capital or military strength – it is perception, reputation, and trust.

It is against this backdrop that Carmelo Cutuli's *The Art and Science of Crafting a Country's Image: The Essential Toolkit for Transforming National Identity into Global Influence* arrives as more than a timely contribution: it is a working doctrine for modern governance and international relations.

For too long, the discussion of national identity has lacked rigor. Governments and policymakers have routinely conflated the projection of national identity with tourism marketing – reducing millennia of culture, complex economies, and layered social narratives to slogans and logos. Destination marketing has its place in a state's economic machinery, but it is wholly inadequate to the task of building genuine geopolitical influence.

Cutuli moves the conversation decisively forward. Drawing on international relations, behavioral economics, digital communications, and brand management, he dismantles outdated paradigms and replaces them with a coherent, disciplined framework. At its core lies a truth that every modern diplomat and legislator must accept: a country's image is not a veneer to be painted over its flaws. It must be a faithful reflection of authentic identity – one that demands rigorous management, strategic foresight, and continuous cultivation.

As a Senator representing citizens living abroad, I have seen at close quarters how a nation's image operates in practice. A country's reputation does not reside within the walls of its embassies or the halls of its parliament alone; it lives in the daily interactions of its diaspora, the quality of its exported goods, the conduct of its businesses overseas, and the cultural reach of its arts. It is, by nature, a multi-stakeholder phenomenon.

In *The Art and Science of Crafting a Country's Image*, Cutuli captures this complexity. He argues – persuasively – that authentic identity cannot be fabricated; it must be unearthed, understood, and strategically projected. The book offers a clear path through this process, showing how nations can convey their character across highly diverse cultural contexts without losing coherence or credibility.

What distinguishes Cutuli's approach is his integration of behavioral economics. By understanding how international stakeholders – foreign investors, skilled expatriates, tourists, allied governments – perceive and process information, a nation can sharpen its distinctive value proposition. This is not manipulation; it is clarity in a noisy world. It is the difference between a nation's true value being lost in translation and being communicated in terms that resonate with the psychological and cultural realities of its audience.

The theoretical foundations of the book are strong, but its greatest achievement is practical. Cutuli has not written a philosophical treatise on soft power; he has produced a working handbook.

The passage from theory to practice defeats many governments. How does one measure something as intangible as a nation's reputation? Cutuli answers with a clear methodology for assessing where a nation currently stands in global perception. This empirical starting point is essential: without a baseline, any attempt to shape a narrative is navigation without a map.

From there, the toolkit expands. The book examines how to develop distinctive value propositions – how to identify what makes a nation uniquely competitive and how to articulate that advantage with precision. Cutuli also addresses the often-neglected challenge of aligning multi-stakeholder initiatives. In a democratic society, a government cannot impose a single narrative on its corporations, universities, and citizens. It must instead foster conditions in which the varied voices of a nation naturally converge around a cohesive image.

Of particular relevance to the present moment, the book confronts the problem of crisis communications. We live in an age of volatility, where a single misstep or geopolitical friction can reverberate globally in seconds. Cutuli offers strategic guidance on safeguarding a nation's reputation during such episodes, ensuring that long-term equity is not sacrificed to short-term turbulence.

Why should government officials, diplomats, and business leaders invest time and resources in the study of national image? The answer, as this book makes plain, is bound directly to a nation's competitive standing and long-term prosperity. The global competition for mobile resources – foreign direct investment, intellectual capital, high-value tourism, political goodwill – is intensifying.

When a company decides where to build its next research facility, it looks beyond tax incentives to the host nation's reputation for innovation, stability, and rule of law. When first-rate talent chooses where to settle, it gravitates toward nations whose image signals opportunity, openness, and quality of life. When international bodies weigh critical geopolitical decisions, the trust and reputation of the nations involved bear heavily on the outcome.

In this context, the capacity to shape perceptions is not optional; it is a pillar of national security and economic viability.

The Art and Science of Crafting a Country's Image is both an intellectual contribution and a practical necessity. Cutuli has given us a framework for understanding the invisible forces that shape our globalized world – and, more importantly, the tools to act on that understanding.

As someone who has devoted a public career to bridging the distance between my home country and the wider world, I recognize the value of this work. It challenges us to think beyond the superficial marketing tactics of the past and to embrace a more rigorous, more strategic approach to national identity.

I commend this book not only as recommended reading but also as a working instrument for anyone tasked with representing, governing, or conducting business on behalf of a nation. Our national image is among our most valuable, most vulnerable, and most powerful assets. By mastering what these pages set out, we stand a better chance not only of navigating the complexities of the twenty-first century but of leading through them – with influence, authenticity, and lasting prosperity.

The Hon. Dr. Francesco Giacobbe
O.A.M., O.M.R.I., PhD, M.Bus., B.Bus., F.T.I.A., C.T.A., F.I.P.A., J.P., Senator of the Italian Republic.

INTRODUCTION

Long before the word «brand» entered the vocabulary of states, before public relations consultancies drafted strategic narratives for foreign ministries, and long before an algorithm could shape the global perception of a country overnight, nations already possessed reputations. Ancient Athens was famed for its philosophy and feared for its navy. Rome projected its own idea of civilization alongside its legions. Venice traded as much on its aura of sophistication as on its merchant fleet. Reputation, in other words, is not a modern invention – it is one of the oldest and least understood forms of power that nations wield over one another and over themselves.

And yet, despite its antiquity, national reputation remains strangely resistant to systematic understanding. It is spoken of constantly in ministries of foreign affairs, in tourism boards, in export promotion agencies, in consultancies that specialize in «nation branding», and in the editorial rooms of international media. It is measured by indexes, tracked by surveys, celebrated in rankings, and mourned when it collapses. But beneath this frenzy of measurement and management lies a paradox that this book takes as its starting point: a nation's reputation determines an extraordinary range of material outcomes – the premium consumers are willing to pay for its exports, the desirability of its passport, the weight its diplomats carry in multilateral negotiations, the ease with which its universities attract students, the flow of tourists crossing its borders, the willingness of talent and capital to settle within them – and yet no single country fully controls this reputation, no single discipline can fully explain it, and no communication campaign, however well-funded or brilliantly executed, can substitute for the substance that ultimately shapes it.

This is the territory the book seeks to map. Not to promise mastery over it, because mastery is precisely what cannot be promised, but to offer an honest account of how national reputation forms, how it operates, and how it occasionally – sometimes spectacularly – collapses. There is a reason the literature on national image is fragmented. The subject sits at the intersection of too many fields, each of which has claimed a portion of it while leaving the rest untouched.

Public relations practitioners approach the nation as a client to be advised, focusing on messaging, stakeholder management, and crisis response. Marketers and place branders treat it as a product to be positioned in the global marketplace of attention, applying segmentation and differentiation frameworks borrowed from corporate strategy. Public diplomacy scholars, often working within or adjacent to foreign ministries, frame it as an instrument of statecraft, a complement to traditional diplomacy aimed at foreign publics rather than foreign governments. Political scientists, particularly those working in the tradition Joseph Nye inaugurated with the concept of *soft power*, see it as a resource that shapes international outcomes without recourse to coercion or payment. Sociologists and cultural theorists, following the idea that nations are *imagined communities*, study how national identity is manufactured and reproduced in the first place – the raw material, as it were, from which reputation is made. Semioticians examine the signs, symbols, and codes through which a nation becomes legible to outsiders. And cultural theorists in the tradition of Stuart Hall remind us that representation is never neutral: every image of a nation carries the traces of the power relations that produced it.

These disciplines rarely speak to each other. A public diplomacy handbook will seldom reference a semiotic analysis of flag iconography. A place branding consultancy will rarely cite the *Stereotype Content Model* from social psychology, even though its own work unknowingly depends on the warmth – competence axes that model describes. A political scientist writing about soft power may be unaware of the specific operational frameworks – Anholt's *Nation Brand Hexagon*, Coombs' *Situational Crisis Communication Theory*, the *FutureBrand Country Index* methodology – that practitioners deploy daily in the field. The result is a literature that is at once voluminous and oddly incomplete: each discipline holds a piece of the puzzle, but the puzzle itself is rarely assembled.

This book is an attempt at that assembly. It is an *essay* in the older sense of the word – an attempt, a try – rather than a definitive treatise. It draws on thinkers from several disciplines and the working instruments they left behind. Its ambition is not to produce a unified theory of national reputation (a task that may be impossible and is certainly premature) but to show that the intersections between these fields are where the real work of understanding happens. The frameworks that practitioners use, the concepts that scholars debate, the intuitions that diplomats rely on – all of them become richer when placed in conversation with one another.

One of the central premises of what follows is that nations exist, for the purposes of their external reputation, primarily as *narratives*. This is not a dismissal of their material reality. Borders are real, institutions are real, economies are real, and the lives of citizens are emphatically real. But the way nations register in the minds of foreigners – the way they become objects of attraction, suspicion, admiration, or indifference – is through stories. Some of these stories a country tells about itself. Others are told *about* it, by neighbors, rivals, former colonies, diaspora communities, journalists, filmmakers, novelists, athletes, tourists, and now, increasingly, by algorithms curating content for audiences no ministry can directly reach.

This narrative character of national reputation has several consequences that run through every chapter of this book. First, it means that a nation's image is always a co-production. No government, however authoritarian, fully authors the story of its country abroad. Second, it means that national reputation is *historical* – it carries sediments of the past that cannot simply be willed away by present-day communication efforts. A country's colonial history, its wars, its economic crises, its moments of glory and its moments of shame, all leave residues that new messaging must work with or against, but cannot ignore. Third, it means that reputation is *relational*: countries are perceived in contrast and comparison with others, within regional groupings, civilizational categories, and the implicit hierarchies of a global imaginary that is itself unevenly distributed.

The insight that the nation is an *imagined community* applies here with a twist. If nations are imagined into being domestically through shared media, language, rituals, and education, they are re-imagined internationally through a different set of instruments: news cycles, cultural exports, diplomatic performances, tourism imagery, diaspora influence, international sports, global consumer brands that bear national markers, and, crucially, the daily actions of a country's own government as observed by the world. The international imagination of a nation is thinner than its domestic imagination – outsiders know less, care less, and attend less – but it is also, for that reason, more volatile. A single event can reshape it dramatically, for better or worse, in ways that domestic national identity, anchored by decades of lived experience, rarely permits.

Every serious treatment of national reputation eventually runs up against a tension that most accounts try to resolve in one direction or another. The first direction treats reputation as fundamentally *constructed* – a matter of communication, symbolism, and strategic framing that skilled professionals can shape and reshape according to plan. The second direction treats reputation as fundamentally *determined by reality* – by what a country actually does, produces, and is, such that communication is at best a marginal adjustment to forces well beyond its reach.

Both positions contain truth, and both are incomplete. The first is the temptation of the consultant, who sells the promise that perception can be engineered. The second is the temptation of the realist, who dismisses image management as cosmetic and insists that substance is the only thing that matters. In practice, the field operates in the space between these positions, and the honest practitioner or scholar must learn to hold that space open.

The central argument of this book – pursued through every chapter, though stated in different ways depending on the material at hand – is that a nation's reputation is at once *constructed and real, manageable and uncontrollable, an instrument of power and a mirror of identity.* It is constructed because it is made of signs, stories, and perceptions that can be shaped; it is real because those perceptions have material consequences and because they depend on actual national conduct. It is manageable because skilled communication and strategic action can shift it at the margins, sometimes significantly; it is uncontrollable because it depends on the attention, interpretations, and agendas of millions of actors no government can command. It is an instrument of power because it can be deployed to advance national interests abroad; but it is also a mirror of identity, because the stories a country tells the world are inevitably entangled with the stories it tells itself, and the external image reflects back onto domestic self-understanding in ways that are not always welcome.

Holding this tension open – rather than collapsing it toward either pole – is, in my view, the only honest way to think about the image of a country in the world. Much of the existing literature leans in one direction or the other, either overselling the power of branding or dismissing it as epiphenomenal. This book tries to resist both temptations.

Practitioners looking for a toolkit will find one here. The book names and uses the operational frameworks that have shaped the field over the past three decades. These frameworks, however, appear in the chapters that follow only where the argument requires them, because the danger of any toolkit is that it can substitute for thinking. The ambition here is the opposite: that these instruments support thinking, as part of a broader argument that they neither exhaust nor constrain.

This is why the book refuses to be only a manual. Manuals assume that the problems are already well-defined and that the reader needs only the right instrument to solve them. The problems of national reputation are rarely so neat. They arrive entangled with history, ideology, economic interest, domestic politics, and the unpredictable rhythms of the international news cycle. A useful book on this subject must help the reader *think*, not merely act – and must respect the fact that the best practitioners in this field are invariably those who have internalized the concepts deeply enough to know when to deviate from them.

This third edition adds a new chapter addressing what no book on national reputation written today can afford to ignore: the transformations that the last two decades of technological change have brought to the field. Any account that overlooked them would be obsolete before its ink dried. The rise of global social platforms has shattered the twentieth-century model in which national image-making was primarily a matter of managing relations with foreign correspondents, cultural attachés, and a relatively small set of gatekeeping institutions. Today, a nation's image is constructed continuously, in real time, across dozens of platforms, by millions of actors – tourists with smartphones, diaspora TikTok creators, foreign influencers, domestic propagandists, hostile disinformation operations, international journalists, and ordinary citizens of the country itself, whose daily conduct becomes globally visible in ways their grandparents could not have imagined.

The arrival of generative artificial intelligence has added another layer. Large language models now mediate a significant portion of how people learn about countries they have never visited; image-generation models produce visual representations of nations at industrial scale; recommendation algorithms decide which aspects of a country's reality surface for which audiences. The old question of «how do we communicate our country to the world» has been joined by a newer and stranger question: how do we ensure that the machines mediating global perception represent our country accurately, fairly, and in ways aligned with our interests – when we neither built those machines nor control their training data?

These developments do not render the older frameworks obsolete, but they do change the conditions under which those frameworks operate. Chapters of this book address these changes directly, not as a futurological supplement but as a constitutive part of the contemporary reality of national image-making.

The book is addressed to several audiences at once, and it makes no apology for this. It is for practitioners – communication strategists in foreign ministries, place branding consultants, public diplomacy officers, tourism board directors, export promotion agency staff, and the consultancies that advise them – who want a framework broader than the toolkits they have inherited. It is for scholars working in the overlapping fields of international communication, political science, and cultural studies, who may find the bridge-building between disciplines useful for their own research. It is for journalists covering international affairs who notice that the way countries are reported on has patterns that deserve scrutiny. And it is for the informed general reader who has ever wondered why some countries seem to punch above their weight in the global imagination while others, equally deserving, remain invisible or misunderstood.

Writing for multiple audiences is always a risk; each reader may find passages pitched too high or too low. But the subject itself demands this, because national reputation is not a specialist concern. It shapes the lives of citizens who never think about it and whose fates are nevertheless tied to it. An exporter whose goods are judged by their country of origin, an engineer applying for a visa at a foreign consulate, a student seeking admission to a university abroad, a hotelier whose season depends on a news cycle beyond her control – all are, in various ways, inhabitants of their country's international image, even if the vocabulary of «nation branding» would strike them as abstract.

Finally, a word about the spirit in which this book is written. Those who work on national reputation professionally – as consultants, diplomats, communication officers, or scholars – are sometimes tempted by the grandiosity their subject invites. To speak of «shaping the image of a nation in the world» is to speak of something large, and the rhetoric of the field can easily tip into the rhetoric of omnipotence.

The truth is more modest. Nations have reputations that precede any particular effort to manage them, reputations rooted in centuries of history and in the daily conduct of their citizens and governments. Communication professionals contribute at the margins, and those margins matter, but they are margins. The best work in this field is done by people who understand the limits of their craft and who resist the temptation to promise more than it can deliver.

This book tries to honor that modesty while still taking the craft seriously. National reputation is worth thinking about carefully, not because it can be engineered, but because the effort to understand it better – to see more clearly how it forms, operates, and occasionally collapses – is itself a contribution to the quality of the international conversation in which all nations now, inescapably, participate.

The chapters that follow are offered in that spirit.

CHAPTER 1
THE NATION
AS NARRATIVE

WHAT, EXACTLY, IS A NATION?

B efore speaking about how nations are communicated, projected, or "branded" on the world stage, we must first confront a more basic question – one that the practitioners of reputation management are often too busy to ask: "what, exactly, is a nation?"[1] The assumption running through most professional discourse on country image is that nations are simply there, sitting on the map like geographical facts, waiting to be dressed up or translated for foreign audiences. This book rejects that assumption from its opening pages. Nations are not landscapes with borders drawn around them, nor are they ancient essences passed down unchanged from some mythical origin. They are ongoing collective narratives, continuously produced and reproduced through language, ritual, institutions, and media. They are "stories a population tells itself about itself"[2] – stories so thoroughly woven into daily life that their constructed character becomes invisible.

---

1. The "modernist" school of nationalism – which includes Anderson, Gellner, and Hobsbawm – holds that nations and nationalism are products of modernity created for political and economic ends, in contrast with primordialists, who believe nations have existed since early human history. See Anderson, Benedict. *Imagined Communities: Reflections on the Origin and Spread of Nationalism*. Rev. ed., Verso, 2006.
2. This formulation reflects the now-standard constructivist position that nations are not

This has enormous consequences for everything that follows in this book. Nation branding, public diplomacy, soft-power campaigns[3], tourism promotion, cultural export strategies – none of these activities begin from a blank page. They inherit a text already centuries in the making. They modify, emphasize, and sometimes attempt to redirect a narrative that was in progress long before any consultant was commissioned or any slogan approved. The communicator who fails to understand this will spend considerable resources producing campaigns that feel imposed, artificial, or ideologically motivated – and will wonder why foreign audiences remain unmoved while domestic publics grow resentful.

To establish the conceptual ground for everything that follows, this chapter draws on three foundational thinkers: Benedict Anderson, Eric Hobsbawm, and Michael Billig[4]. Read together rather than in isolation, they deliver a single practical lesson: the raw material of national image-making is always political, always contested, and always older than any strategy designed to shape it. This is deliberately the only chapter of this book that introduces no operational instrument, no framework, no checklist. Before we discuss tools, we must settle what those tools will be working on. The question of what a nation is must be answered in its own terms before the question of how to manage its reputation can be meaningfully posed.

---

ancient communities united by history, blood, language, culture, or territory, as nationalists often claim, but the distinctly modern imagination of a state's population as constituting such an originary community produced by nationalism. See Anderson, Benedict. *Imagined Communities: Reflections on the Origin and Spread of Nationalism*. Rev. ed., Verso, 2006, pp. 5–7.

3. The concept of "soft power" was popularized by Joseph Nye in his 1990 book *Bound to Lead: The Changing Nature of American Power*, where he argued that the ability of one country to get other countries to want what it wants might be called co-optive or soft power, in contrast with the hard or command power of ordering others to do what it wants. See Nye, Joseph S. *Bound to Lead: The Changing Nature of American Power*. Basic Books, 1990, pp. 31–32.

4. These three authors are conventionally cited together as the founding corpus of the modernist/constructivist reading of the nation. See Anderson, Benedict. *Imagined Communities: Reflections on the Origin and Spread of Nationalism*. Rev. ed., Verso, 2006; Hobsbawm, Eric, and Terence Ranger, editors. *The Invention of Tradition*. Cambridge UP, 1983; Billig, Michael. *Banal Nationalism*. SAGE, 1995.

1.1 THE NATION AS A MODERN INVENTION

The first and most counterintuitive fact about the modern nation-state is that it is modern. Despite the rhetoric of "ancient peoples" and "thousand-year histories" that fills national speeches and tourism brochures, the nation-state as we know it – a sovereign political community of formally equal citizens bound by a standardized vernacular, a shared media sphere, and a shared sense of horizontal belonging – is a product of the late eighteenth and nineteenth centuries. It co-evolved with print capitalism[5], mass literacy, industrialization, standing bureaucracies, and the standardization of vernacular languages. It is not the survival of something immemorial; it is one of modernity's most consequential inventions.

Before the national age, the primary political loyalties of most human beings were not national. They were dynastic, religious, municipal, or local. A peasant in seventeenth-century Burgundy was a subject of his lord and, more distantly, of a king; he belonged to a parish, a village, a trade. The abstract proposition that he was part of a horizontal "French people," equal in dignity and destiny to a merchant in Marseille or a weaver in Lille, would have been unintelligible to him. The template of the nation as a political community of equal citizens – replacing subjecthood with nationality[6] as the primary civic identity – was forged in the revolutionary moments of the late eighteenth century, most decisively in the American and French Revolutions. From there it spread, often by force and often by imitation, across Europe, the Americas, and eventually the globe.

The borders that today seem to divide peoples naturally are, upon

---

5. According to Anderson, the creation of imagined communities became possible because of "print capitalism": capitalist entrepreneurs printed their books and media in the vernacular in order to maximize circulation, so that readers speaking various local dialects became able to understand each other and a common discourse emerged. Anderson argues that this process gave rise to the earliest modern national communities first in the Americas and then in Europe. See Anderson, Benedict. *Imagined Communities: Reflections on the Origin and Spread of Nationalism*. Rev. ed., Verso, 2006, pp. 37–46.

6. For Anderson, the imagined community is sovereign because its legitimacy is not derived from divinity as kingship is – the nation is its own authority, founded in its own name, and it invents its own people, which it deems citizens – and it can be considered a community because it implies a deep horizontal comradeship that knits together all citizens irrespective of their class, color, or race. See "Imagined Community." *Oxford Reference*.

examination, political decisions. They were drawn by treaties, wars, colonial administrators, and bureaucratic convenience. They shape identity as much as they reflect it, and their contingency becomes visible whenever we look at them historically. The borders that today separate neighboring nations – whether in Europe, Asia, Africa, or the Americas – are never natural facts. Each is an artifact of specific human decisions at specific moments, most of them recent.

For the communicator, recognizing the modernity of the nation-form is the first intellectual defense against a common trap: naturalization. This is the tendency to treat a recent political construction as though it were an eternal, self-evident given – to speak of "the national character" or "the national spirit" of any given country as though such things existed prior to and independently of the political and cultural processes that produced them. Naturalization is seductive because it simplifies; it offers the reassuring sense that one is working with a fixed object. But it is also the surest route to strategic error. A communicator who mistakes construction for nature will be systematically blind to the levers through which national image actually moves.

1.2 IMAGINED COMMUNITIES: BENEDICT ANDERSON

No single thinker has done more to clarify the peculiar nature of national belonging than Benedict Anderson, whose 1983 book *Imagined Communities* gave the field its most productive working definition. A nation, Anderson argued, is "an imagined political community – and imagined as both inherently limited and sovereign"[7]. It is imagined because no member will ever meet, know, or even hear of most of the other members, yet in the mind of each lives an image of their communion. A Colombian will never meet the vast majority of other Colombians, yet the sense of

---

7. The original formulation appears in Anderson (1983): the nation is an imagined political community that is inherently limited in scope and sovereign in nature – "imagined" because the actuality of even the smallest nation exceeds what it is possible for a single person to know. See Anderson, Benedict. *Imagined Communities: Reflections on the Origin and Spread of Nationalism.* Verso, 1983, p. 6.

belonging to a common Colombian "we" is vivid, emotionally charged, and capable of mobilizing profound sacrifice.

How was this act of collective imagination made possible on such a scale? Anderson's answer points to print capitalism. The mass production of books and, above all, newspapers in standardized vernacular languages created the material conditions under which dispersed populations could come to conceive of themselves as contemporaries – strangers moving through the same events, the same time, the same narrative present. The daily newspaper ritual, in which millions of unconnected individuals consume the same content at roughly the same moment, functions as a kind of secular liturgy. Anderson recalls Hegel's observation that "newspapers serve modern man as a substitute for morning prayers"[8].

It is essential to insist on a point Anderson himself stressed and that is frequently misunderstood. "Imagined" does not mean "unreal." Imagined communities are among the most powerfully real phenomena in modern history. They raise armies, fund infrastructure, enforce borders, tax populations, educate children, and reshape individual biographies. The fact that a community is imagined tells us something about *how* it is constituted, not *whether* it exists or matters. It exists precisely because it is imagined, and it matters because that imagining has been institutionalized in schools, constitutions, currencies, passports, and commemorative calendars.

For the practitioner of nation reputation, Anderson's insight carries a direct operational consequence. Foreign audiences never approach a country empty-handed. They arrive with their own imagined version of it already structured in mind – assembled from films, novels, journalism, tourism marketing, the memories of diasporas, and the vague residue of

---

8. The full passage reads: "The significance of this mass ceremony—Hegel observed that newspapers serve modern man as a substitute for morning prayers—is paradoxical. It is performed in silent privacy, in the lair of the skull. Yet each communicant is well aware that the ceremony he performs is being replicated simultaneously by thousands (or millions) of others of whose existence he is confident, yet of whose identity he has not the slightest notion." See Anderson, Benedict. *Imagined Communities: Reflections on the Origin and Spread of Nationalism*. Rev. ed., Verso, 2006, p. 35. Anderson does not provide a precise philological reference for the Hegelian passage; the formula has become proverbial, but its exact location within Hegel's corpus remains a matter of scholarly debate.

history lessons – and any communication strategy will be processed against that prior image.

1.3 THE INVENTION OF TRADITION: HOBSBAWM AND RANGER

If Anderson explains how modern nations come to be imagined, Eric Hobsbawm and Terence Ranger, in their 1983 collection *The Invention of Tradition*[9], explain how those imaginings acquire the patina of antiquity. Their central claim is historically precise and politically unsettling: many of the traditions we experience as ancient – among the examples Hobsbawm and Ranger examine are the Scottish kilt as national dress[10], the pageantry of the British monarchy[11], the ceremonial uniforms of European armies, and the fixed repertoires of national anthems and founding commemorations – were consciously designed in the course of the nineteenth century, and similar processes can be documented in virtually every modern nation-state.

The function of these inventions was rarely decorative. They served to establish authority, manufacture social cohesion, and legitimate political arrangements through appeal to a past that had been either reconstructed from fragments or fabricated outright. Rituals, dress codes, official histo-

---

9.   The concept was highlighted in the 1983 book *The Invention of Tradition*, edited by Eric Hobsbawm and Terence Ranger, whose introduction argues that many "traditions" which "appear or claim to be old are often quite recent in origin and sometimes invented." See Hobsbawm, Eric, and Terence Ranger, editors. *The Invention of Tradition*. Cambridge UP, 1983, p. 1.

10. In his chapter for *The Invention of Tradition*, Hugh Trevor-Roper argues that the distinctive national apparatus of the Scots – kilt, tartan, bagpipe – to which they ascribe great antiquity, is in fact largely modern, developed after the Union with England as a sort of protest, and largely unknown in its current form before the eighteenth century. See Trevor-Roper, Hugh. "The Invention of Tradition: The Highland Tradition of Scotland." *The Invention of Tradition*, edited by Eric Hobsbawm and Terence Ranger, Cambridge UP, 1983, pp. 15–41.

11. As David Cannadine demonstrates in his chapter of the same volume, much of what today appears as the ancient pageantry of the British monarchy is in fact a ritual repertoire consolidated only from around 1870 onward. See Cannadine, David. "The Context, Performance and Meaning of Ritual: The British Monarchy and the 'Invention of Tradition,' c. 1820–1977." *The Invention of Tradition*, edited by Eric Hobsbawm and Terence Ranger, Cambridge UP, 1983, pp. 101–164.

ries, and public monuments wove populations that had recently been strangers into a single narrative fabric. A new kingdom, a new republic, a newly independent state needed the gravitas of continuity, and if continuity could not be found, it could be made.

Hobsbawm and Ranger are careful, and the communicator should be equally careful, to resist the cynical reading. Invention is rarely forgery in the sense of fraud. The designers of invented traditions often believed themselves to be recovering something lost rather than creating from nothing. They saw themselves as archaeologists of identity, restoring a submerged authenticity. That self-understanding matters, because it explains the moral seriousness with which these traditions were constructed and why they took root so deeply. Once a tradition is established, the memory of its invention fades. It comes to feel authentic, inherited, self-evident. The decisive move is the one that converts artifact into identity.

For reputation work, the implication is that the communicator is always working on material that is neither wholly authentic nor wholly artificial, but historically layered. A national symbol that a consultant might be tempted to dismiss as "constructed" is no less real in its emotional force for having been constructed. Conversely, a symbol that a client insists is "timeless" may well date from a specific parliamentary committee in 1887. Understanding this layering – which elements were made, when, by whom, to solve which political problem – is not academic trivia. It is the diagnostic work that separates competent strategy from improvisation.

1.4 BANAL NATIONALISM: MICHAEL BILLIG

Anderson and Hobsbawm describe the foundations of national identity. Michael Billig, in his 1995 book *Banal Nationalism*[12], describes its daily maintenance. Billig's great contribution was to draw a distinction between

---

12. The term derives from Michael Billig's 1995 book of the same name and is intended to be understood critically. The volume has become one of the most widely cited contributions to the study of everyday nationalism. See Billig, Michael. *Banal Nationalism*. SAGE, 1995.

"hot" nationalism[13] – the nationalism of flags raised in crisis, of ethnic mobilization, of parades, wars, and secession movements – and the quieter, continuous, almost invisible nationalism that reproduces national belonging every day in established states.

Banal nationalism operates in weather maps that assume a national territory[14], in sports coverage that distinguishes "our" athletes from the rest, in the deictic "we" of political rhetoric that silently presumes a national subject addressing itself, in the iconography of currency, in the layout of the national news section of a newspaper. It functions in the unremarkable flag flying above a post office, unnoticed until a foreigner points it out. Its power lies in its invisibility. Because banal nationalism operates below the threshold of critical attention, it reproduces the nation as a taken-for-granted framework of perception rather than as a contested claim.

Billig's insight corrects a common error in popular analysis: the tendency to imagine that national identity is an episodic phenomenon acti-vated at moments of crisis or celebration and dormant otherwise. On the contrary, national identity is the continuous background of political, cultural, and commercial life in modern states. Citizens are "flagged" constantly, unobtrusively, in the ordinary texture of their media envi-ronment.

This has two major consequences for reputation management. First, much of what shapes a country's image – both at home and abroad – oper-ates below the level of conscious communication and therefore lies largely outside direct strategic control. The way a national broadcaster organizes its weather map, the habitual framings of sports journalism, the visual

---

13. Billig used the term banal nationalism to describe nationalism that existed as an under-lying force in everyday life, rather than one that fueled an extreme push for change; he did not view it as a harmless expression of patriotic pride, but as a latent force embedded in the routines of everyday life, liable to be mobilized in moments of national crisis. See Billig, Michael. *Banal Nationalism*. SAGE, 1995, pp. 5–12, 43–59.
14. Examples of banal nationalism include the use of flags in everyday contexts, sporting events, national songs, symbols on money, popular expressions, the implied togetherness of the national press, and divisions into "domestic" and "international" news – symbols most effective because of their constant repetition and almost subliminal nature. See Billig, Michael. *Banal Nationalism*. SAGE, 1995, pp. 93–127 (ch. "Flagging the Homeland Daily").

conventions of banknotes, the cadence of official speech – all of this is doing reputational work, usually without any coordinating authority. Second, because banal nationalism is the medium through which most national identity is actually experienced, the most effective communication strategies often work *with*, rather than against, these quiet patterns. A campaign that ignores banal registers in favor of loud symbolic gestures will feel thin and declarative; one that modulates the everyday textures through which a nation is already narrated will feel grounded and authentic.

1.5 WHO HAS THE RIGHT TO TELL THE NATION

No narrative is neutral, and national narratives are among the most politically loaded stories in circulation. Every telling of a nation privileges certain voices and silences others. Dominant groups speak over minorities. The political and cultural center frames the periphery. Official memory edits out subaltern recollection. The history of a modern nation, as taught in its schools and celebrated in its monuments, is always a selection – and a selection is always a politics.

Counter-narratives are therefore a permanent feature of the national text. Diasporic communities remember differently from metropolitan elites. Indigenous peoples preserve accounts that directly contradict the heroic self-image embedded in dominant national histories. Dissidents, exiles, suppressed political movements, and forgotten regional cultures keep alive versions of the national past that the official story has marginalized. These counter-narratives do not go away because they are excluded; they circulate in family memory, in vernacular media, in academic scholarship, in artistic production, and – increasingly – in global digital networks.

The very claim of "authenticity" attached to a national narrative is itself a political construct. Authenticity, in this domain, is not an objective property of a story but a marker of who currently holds narrative authority. When a regime insists that its account of the nation is the authentic one, what is being asserted is a power relation, not a historical verdict. This is visible whenever political transition occurs: the overthrow of a regime, the end of a colonial relationship, the democratic opening of a closed society – each brings with it a rapid renegotiation of which stories now count as the true story of the nation.

Two historical developments have sharply intensified this dynamic. Globalization has exposed national self-descriptions to constant external scrutiny, comparison, and challenge. Digital media have radically democratized the production of national narratives, eroding the historical monopoly that states enjoyed over their own self-representation. A ministry of foreign affairs can no longer assume that its official framing of the country will dominate the informational environment. A single viral video produced by a dissident, a diaspora activist, or an investigative journalist can reach larger audiences than a state-funded campaign.

For the communicator, this means that the question of *who narrates a nation* is not a matter of abstract political theory. It is a live, operational question with direct consequences for how reputation forms, stabilizes, and changes. Strategies that depend on narrative monopoly are strategies built on a foundation that no longer exists.

1.6 WORKING WITH A STORY ALREADY IN PROGRESS

Everything in this chapter converges on a single pragmatic conclusion, one that will govern the approach of this book. Any attempt to shape a nation's image is an intervention into a pre-existing narrative ecosystem, not a blank-slate construction available for strategic authorship. The communicator arrives late to a text written over centuries by historical events, political struggles, invented traditions, daily banal reproduction, and competing counter-narratives. The tools described in the chapters to come are not authoring tools. They are editorial tools, curatorial tools, and diplomatic tools.

Effective intervention begins with diagnosis. The communicator must learn to distinguish between stable narrative layers – deep historical imagery, long-settled associations, iconic landscapes and figures – and volatile ones, such as current events, recent political shifts, and moments of reputational crisis. A campaign that confuses these layers, treating the volatile as permanent or the stable as easily revised, is a campaign designed to fail.

Ignoring existing narrative structures is the most common cause of the artificial, imposed, or ideologically driven tone that afflicts so many national image campaigns. When a strategy contradicts the story the population already tells about itself, it generates resistance at home and skepticism abroad. When it bears no recognizable relationship to what foreign audiences already imagine about the country, it is simply ignored. The productive path runs in the opposite direction: first listen to the existing story – its heroes, traumas, achievements, contradictions, silences – before adding anything new to it.

This requires a kind of professional humility that is not always welcome in the industry. The communicator is not the author of a national narrative. The communicator is a late and marginal contributor to a collective text that has been written, rewritten, and contested for generations, and that will continue to be written long after any particular campaign has run its course. Accepting this position is not a diminishment of the work. On the contrary, it is the precondition for doing the work well. It is the difference between a contribution that deepens a nation's story and an advertisement that briefly interrupts it.

The chapters that follow will introduce the operational tools of that contribution: the frameworks, methods, and tactics through which national identity is translated into global influence. But none of those tools will function as intended unless they are used with the understanding established here. The nation is a narrative. It was narrated before we arrived, it is being narrated around us as we work, and it will continue to be narrated after we are gone. Our job is to intervene in that narration with intelligence, respect, and strategic purpose – not to pretend we are writing on an empty page.

CHAPTER 2
THE IDENTITY
OF A COUNTRY
WHO WE ARE AND
HOW WE KNOW IT

A country's identity is never a single, stable thing. It is the product of an ongoing negotiation between three parties that rarely agree: the citizens who live inside the country and hold some image of what it is[1], the institutions that officially represent the country to the world, and the foreign audiences whose perceptions ultimately determine how the country is received on the international stage. These three parties operate with different information, different interests, and different time horizons. Their images of the nation overlap but never coincide. Managing a country's reputation, therefore, begins not with a campaign but with a diagnostic – an honest attempt to map where these images match, where they diverge, and why.

This chapter introduces the two instruments that have done most to shape how professionals think about national identity over the past quarter-century. The first is Simon Anholt's Nation Brand Hexagon[2], which

---

1. Anderson's seminal formulation of the nation as an "imagined community" grounds this observation: "the members of even the smallest nation will never know most of their fellow-members, meet them, or even hear of them, yet in the minds of each lives the image of their communion" (p. 6). See Anderson, Benedict. *Imagined Communities: Reflections on the Origin and Spread of Nationalism*. Rev. ed., Verso, 2006 (first published 1983).
2. Anholt coined the term "nation brand" in the late 1990s, inaugurating a new field of

decomposes the elusive notion of national reputation into six interacting dimensions and thereby makes it analyzable. The second is the Country of Origin Effect[3], a body of findings from marketing research that captures the way every exported product carries its nationality as a silent reputational signal, whether the country wants it to or not. Taken together, these two instruments do something that intuition alone cannot: they turn the vague, emotional category of "how our country is seen" into a set of concrete, testable questions.

The chapter's aim is not to offer a formula. It is to equip the reader with the conceptual instruments needed to diagnose what kind of identity problem – or identity asset – a country is actually dealing with. Before choosing any strategy, a practitioner must know what is being worked on, what plane of reality is in question, and which dimensions are susceptible to communicative intervention at all.

2.1 SELF-PERCEPTION AND EXTERNAL PERCEPTION

The first structural fact of national reputation is that every nation holds an image of itself that rarely coincides with the image others hold of it. This asymmetry is not a malfunction. It is not evidence that something has gone wrong with communication. It is a constitutive feature of the entire domain, built into the conditions under which self-perception and external perception are produced.

Self-perception is generated from the inside. It is informed by lived experience, schooling, civic rituals, political debate, family memory, and the dense texture of daily life within the nation's borders. It tends, unsurprisingly, to emphasize ideals, historical achievements, and aspirational

---

research and practice. See Anholt, Simon. "Nation-Brands of the Twenty-First Century." *Journal of Brand Management*, vol. 5, no. 6, 1998, pp. 395–406; and, for the systematic exposition, Anholt, Simon. *Competitive Identity: The New Brand Management for Nations, Cities and Regions*. Palgrave Macmillan, 2007.

3. The foundational empirical study is generally attributed to Schooler, R. D. "Product Bias in the Central American Common Market." *Journal of Marketing Research*, vol. 2, no. 4, 1965, pp. 394–397. For a complementary early formulation focused on consumer perception, see also Dichter, Ernest. "The World Customer." *Harvard Business Review*, vol. 40, no. 4, 1962, pp. 113–122.

identity. Citizens know their country in detail, including its failures, but they also know the full cultural and moral context in which those failures sit. They grant themselves complexity.

External perception is generated from the outside and under very different conditions[4]. Foreign audiences do not live inside the national experience; they meet the country through narrow and often accidental channels – a news report, a sporting event, a tourist encounter, a product on a shelf, a film, a diplomatic incident. These channels are fragmentary, filtered, and heavily biased toward whatever is dramatic, visible, or exportable. External perception therefore tends to reduce complexity to a small number of salient, often inherited traits. The country becomes a shorthand: a cuisine, a conflict, a leader, a landscape, a cliché.

The gap between internal and external image is not a problem to be collapsed. It is a field to be mapped and understood. Some of the most common strategic errors in this profession come from a failure to make peace with the gap. Nations invest enormous communicative effort into dimensions that matter domestically – historical anniversaries, internal political achievements, constitutional milestones – but which are invisible or irrelevant to foreign audiences. Conversely, they neglect dimensions that are decisive abroad because those dimensions feel trivial or embarrassing at home. The first diagnostic task of any serious reflection on national reputation is therefore to map this asymmetry honestly. Without defensiveness about the existence of the gap, and without illusions about its size. Only once the map is drawn can the question of strategy even be posed.

2.2 THE NATION BRAND HEXAGON: AN ANATOMY

When Simon Anholt began his work on national reputation in the late 1990s and early 2000s, he faced a practical difficulty that still shapes the field. "National image" is an intuitive concept that resists analysis. Practi-

---

4. On how print media and narrow communicative channels construct external images of the nation, see Anderson's analysis of the way media, maps, censuses, and museums target and define mass audiences through dominant images and language. Anderson, Benedict. *Imagined Communities*. Rev. ed., Verso, 2006, ch. 10 ("Census, Map, Museum"), pp. 163–185.

tioners would speak of a country's reputation as though it were a single grade – good or bad, rising or falling – when in reality reputation is distributed unevenly across many distinct surfaces of contact between a country and the world. To measure or manage it, those surfaces had to be separated.

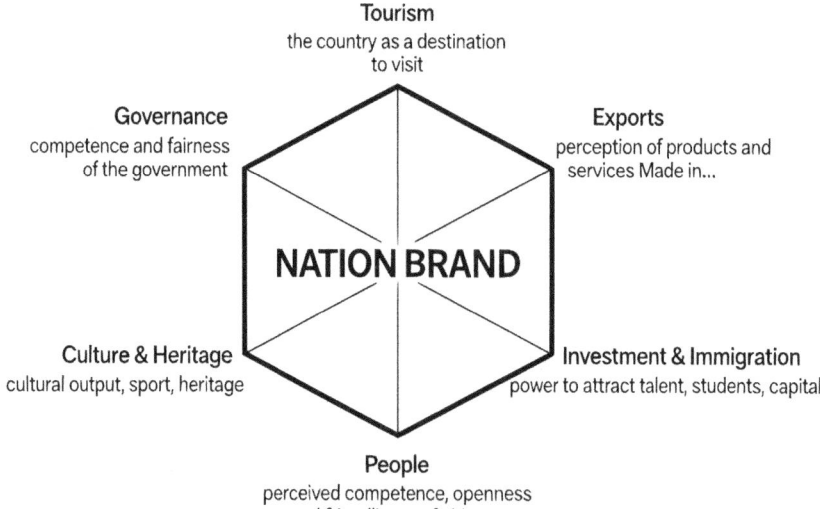

Fig. 1 - Schematic representation of the Nation Brand Hexagon developed by Simon Anholt.

The tool Anholt proposed to do this work was the Nation Brand Hexagon. It identifies six dimensions through which countries are perceived internationally[5]: *tourism* (how attractive the country is as a destination), *exports* (what the country makes and how its goods are regarded), *governance* (the perceived quality of its political institutions and conduct), *people* (the perceived character and competence of its population), *culture and heritage* (its contribution to global culture, past and present), and

___

5. The Anholt–Ipsos Nation Brands Index measures the international reputation of nations by combining six dimensions: exports, governance, culture, people, tourism, and immigration and investment. See *Anholt-Ipsos Nation Brands Index (NBI): Taking Your Reputation Places*. Ipsos, 2021.

immigration and investment (its desirability as a place to invest, work, or settle).

The conceptual power of the Hexagon lies precisely in its comprehensiveness. It captures the fact that national reputation is multidimensional and cannot be reduced to a single slogan, logo, or positioning line. Each of the six dimensions operates semi-independently. A country can score high on culture and low on governance, as several states have demonstrated for years. It can score high on exports and low on tourism, as industrial powers sometimes do. It can score high on people and low on investment, producing a profile beloved by travelers but avoided by capital. The result is that every nation has not a grade but a composite profile – a shape, not a number[6].

It is crucial to understand that the Hexagon works first as a diagnostic instrument and only secondarily as a strategic tool. Its initial function is to force an honest picture of where a country stands on each dimension. Only once that picture is drawn does it become meaningful to ask what can be improved, what can be emphasized, and what must simply be accepted.

The Hexagon also delivers an uncomfortable truth that this book will return to repeatedly. Communication cannot substitute for substance[7]. If governance is weak, no campaign will fix the governance dimension of the Hexagon. If exports are shoddy, no advertising will durably raise the exports score. The model's honesty lies in exposing this: the dimensions of national reputation are anchored in reality, and reputation work that ignores the underlying substance eventually meets the wall of direct experience.

---

6. For the evolution of the Hexagon into the Competitive Identity model, which adds the dimension of coordinated policy and strategy, see Anholt's later development, to be read not as a replacement but as a completion of the earlier Nation Brand Hexagon. Anholt, Simon. *Competitive Identity: The New Brand Management for Nations, Cities and Regions*. Palgrave Macmillan, 2007, ch. 2.

7. This echoes Aronczyk's critical finding that the marketization of national identity reinforces existing inequalities when branding is used to displace substantive reform. Aronczyk, Melissa. *Branding the Nation: The Global Business of National Identity*. Oxford UP, 2013.

2.3 THE SIX DIMENSIONS OF THE MODEL

Like every analytical model, the Hexagon both illuminates and obscures. Its value depends on using it with awareness of both sides.

What it reveals is the composite nature of national reputation. It makes explicit that a country is not one thing in the global mind but several things at once, and that those things are rated separately. This is a decisive improvement over the pre-Anholt habit of speaking about "image" as a mood. It allows the practitioner to identify precisely which dimensions are carrying the reputation and which are dragging it down. It also allows for targeted investment. A country that discovers, through Hexagon-type research, that its culture dimension is far stronger than its exports dimension has actionable information: it can consider leveraging cultural reputation to lift the commercial one, rather than spending resources on a generic image campaign that addresses neither.

What the model hides, or at least under-weights, is the structural politics of perception itself. The Hexagon treats the six dimensions as formally equal, but they are not experientially equal. For some countries, culture carries almost the entire reputational load – think of the way France or Italy are understood globally. For others, governance dominates – Scandinavian countries have built much of their contemporary standing on this axis. For still others, exports do the work – Germany, South Korea, Switzerland. The dimensions are equal in the model; they are unequal in reality, and the weighting varies by audience and by context.

The model also implicitly assumes a rational and reasonably informed observer. In reality, perception is shaped by stereotypes, media framings, affective shortcuts, and the strict limits of global attention. Most foreign publics do not have thought-through evaluations of a country across six dimensions. They have a few images, a few associations, and a general feeling. The Hexagon describes the structure against which that feeling is organized, but it does not describe how the feeling is formed.

There is a further asymmetry the model tends to downplay: some nations are simply granted more complexity in the global imagination than others[8]. Powerful, wealthy, or culturally dominant countries are perceived with nuance. Smaller, poorer, or geopolitically marginal countries are perceived with blunt instruments, regardless of their actual profile. The Hexagon can describe what is perceived, but it cannot by itself explain why some countries are seen at high resolution and others only in silhouette.

Any serious use of the Hexagon must therefore be supplemented by attention to what lies outside its frame: history, affect, media asymmetries, and the politics of global visibility itself.

2.4 THE COUNTRY OF ORIGIN EFFECT

While Anholt was developing tools for the strategic management of national reputation, a parallel and much older body of research in marketing and consumer behavior had been documenting a related phenomenon from a different angle. The Country of Origin Effect, studied in various forms since the 1960s, describes how a product's perceived nationality shapes consumer evaluations[9] of its quality, safety, craftsmanship, and overall desirability.

The effect operates largely below conscious reasoning. It functions as a cognitive shortcut: when a consumer cannot or does not wish to evaluate a product on its individual merits, they attach to it the traits they already associate with its country of origin. A watch described as Swiss is generally perceived as more precise before it has been examined. A car described as German is perceived as better engineered before it has been driven. A handbag described as Italian is perceived as better designed before it has been inspected. These associations may or may not be accu-

---

8. On the asymmetry of global visibility and soft-power resources, see Nye, Joseph S. *Soft Power: The Means to Success in World Politics*. PublicAffairs, 2004. Soft power lies in the ability to attract and persuade, arising from the attractiveness of a country's culture, political ideals, and policies.

9. For a comprehensive meta-analysis quantifying the effect, see Verlegh, Peeter W. J., and Jan-Benedict E. M. Steenkamp. "A Review and Meta-Analysis of Country-of-Origin Research." *Journal of Economic Psychology*, vol. 20, no. 5, 1999, pp. 521–546.

rate in any given case, but the perception does most of the work the marketing department would otherwise need to do on its own.

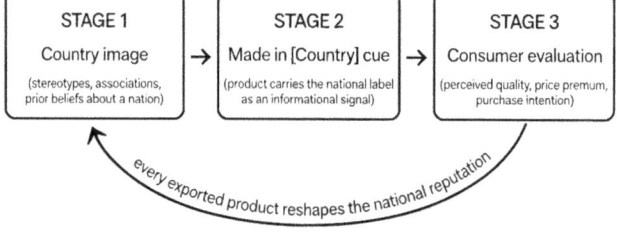

Fig. 2 - Conceptual model of the Country of Origin (COO) effect.

The effect is profoundly asymmetrical. Some origins confer a reputational dividend that functions as a subsidy to every company exporting from that country. *German engineering, Italian design, Japanese precision, French elegance, Swiss reliability* – these are not just stereotypes. They are economic assets, measurable in the price premiums consumers are willing to pay and in the market access exporters enjoy. Other origins carry a persistent liability, regardless of the actual quality of the goods. Excellent products from countries with weak Country of Origin reputations must work harder, price lower, and often rebrand through intermediary markets in order to compete.

For our purposes, the most important implication is the following. The Country of Origin Effect generates a continuous, involuntary form of nation branding. Every exported good carries its origin as a reputational footprint[10], whether or not the country deliberately manages it. Each transaction in which the origin is visible – on a label, in a brand name, in a

---

10. For a book-length treatment integrating COO with nation-branding theory, see Dinnie, Keith. *Nation Branding: Concepts, Issues, Practice*. Butterworth-Heinemann, 2008, ch. 4. Dinnie devotes dedicated chapters to country-of-origin, national identity, and nation branding.

shop's sourcing – is a micro-communication about the nation. Over millions of such transactions, an image is formed or reinforced.

The strategic insight is uncomfortable but clarifying: nation branding happens by default[11]. It is not an optional activity that governments can choose to undertake or ignore. Whether a country has a national branding strategy or not, its products, services, and citizens are transmitting a reputation abroad every day. The real choice is not whether to engage in nation branding, but whether to do so consciously.

2.5 THE GAP BETWEEN BEING, SAYING, AND BEING PERCEIVED

The instruments introduced so far – the Hexagon and the Country of Origin Effect – point toward a deeper structural feature of national reputation that deserves to be stated plainly. Three distinct planes coexist in every national image: what the country actually is (*substance*), what it says about itself (*communication*), and how others perceive it (*reception*).

These three planes never perfectly align. Alignment across all three is the exception, not the rule. Most nations exhibit significant gaps between substance, message, and reception. A country may be genuinely innovative (substance) but unable to tell that story effectively (communication failure). It may tell a compelling story (communication) that does not reach or land with foreign audiences (reception failure). It may be received in ways (reception) that bear little relationship to either its actual character or its intended message – a failure that is usually historical or geopolitical in origin, and only partly amenable to communicative repair.

The distinction matters because the three gaps call for different interventions. Communication can narrow the gap between what is said and what is perceived, because that gap lives inside the communicative field itself. Messaging, media strategy, channel selection, audience segmenta-

---

11. On this involuntary, continuous transmission of national reputation, see Aronczyk's argument that national governments turn to branding consultants to articulate more coherent identities, attract capital, and maintain citizen loyalty – yet the nation is transmitted as a brand regardless of deliberate strategy. Aronczyk, Melissa. *Branding the Nation: The Global Business of National Identity*. Oxford UP, 2013, pp. 3–24.

tion – these are the instruments for closing it. But only substance can narrow the gap between what is said and what actually is. If a country claims to be transparent while its institutions are opaque, no amount of better storytelling will sustainably close that gap. Exposure – through journalism, through tourist experience, through direct business dealings – will eventually catch up with the claim.

Strategic honesty, therefore, begins with diagnosing which gap is largest in a given case. Is the issue that the country is doing remarkable things that it fails to articulate? Is it that it articulates well but cannot reach the right ears? Is it that the underlying reality does not match the ambition of the message? The answer to this question determines whether the work required is primarily communicative, primarily political, primarily structural, or – as is usually the case – some combination of all three, in a specific sequence.

Sustainable reputation lives in the alignment of the three planes. Its absence produces hollow branding that may perform well in the short term but eventually collapses under the pressure of direct exposure. The reputational casualties of the past two decades[12] – countries that invested heavily in image campaigns while allowing their substance to deteriorate – offer a consistent lesson: communication without substance buys time, not reputation.

2.6 PLURAL IDENTITY AND INTERNAL CONFLICT

The analysis so far has, for clarity, spoken of "the country" and "the nation" as though each were a unified speaker with a single identity to project. In reality, no nation speaks with a single voice. Every country contains regional identities that resist the dominance of the capital[13],

---

12. On the critique of nation branding as a superficial substitute for structural reform, see Aronczyk's deconstruction, based on over a decade of research and 100 interviews with practitioners across 12 countries, of the phenomenon of nation brands in the context of nationalism and neoliberalism. Aronczyk, *Branding the Nation*, pp. 25–62.
13. On the fragmentation of national identity in late modernity, see Hall, Stuart. "The Question of Cultural Identity." *Modernity and Its Futures*, edited by Stuart Hall, David Held, and Tony McGrew, Polity Press in association with the Open University, 1992, pp. 274–316. Hall argues that the fully unified, coherent identity is a fantasy: national cultures stitch up internal

generational fractures that produce sharply different visions of the national future, political divisions that extend into incompatible readings of the national past, diasporic perspectives that diverge from those of citizens at home, and minority traditions – linguistic, religious, ethnic – that carry their own accounts of what the nation has been and should be.

The fiction of a unified national identity is itself a political project[14], not a descriptive account. It is the product of centralizing forces – states, educational systems, dominant media – that have historically worked to produce cohesion out of diversity. That project is never completed. It is continuously contested from within the country's own borders. Whoever is writing the official national story at any given moment is doing so against, over, or in uneasy coalition with other storytellers who hold other versions.

Internal disagreement about what the nation is creates a structural ambiguity in how it presents itself externally. The country's external image inherits its internal contradictions. A country that is deeply divided about its colonial past, its religious character, its economic model, or its constitutional identity will find those divisions reappearing in the inconsistency of its international communication. Foreign audiences may not understand the specific debates, but they register the inconsistency, and they often interpret it as unreliability.

The communicator faces a genuine choice between two failure modes. One is to *enforce a single narrative* – picking one version of the nation and projecting it outward as though it were the whole. This produces coherence at the cost of inauthenticity, and it alienates the constituencies whose versions were excluded. The other is to *curate plurality* – attempting to represent the country's internal diversity in its external image. This produces authenticity at the cost of coherence, and it risks

---

divisions, contradictions, and cross-cutting allegiances into one identity, and national identities are formed within representation rather than imprinted in genes.

14. The classic thesis is developed in Hobsbawm and Ranger's argument that many traditions presented as ancient are in fact recent and consciously invented, and that this process is particularly clear in the development of nationalism and national identity. Hobsbawm, Eric, and Terence Ranger, editors. *The Invention of Tradition*. Cambridge UP, 1983.

diluting the identity into a shape that foreign audiences cannot hold in mind.

There is no clean solution, because plural identity is not a communication problem to be solved. It is the reality that any honest national narrative must acknowledge and integrate into its own architecture. The countries that manage this best tend to do two things. They identify a stable core – values, commitments, or characteristics that command broad internal agreement – and project that core with consistency. And they treat internal plurality itself as part of the national story, presenting the country not as a monolith but as a functioning conversation among different voices. This second move converts what would otherwise be a weakness into a feature: the nation is shown as capable of holding difference without disintegrating, which is, in the current global moment, a reputational asset of increasing value[15].

What this chapter has established is the diagnostic terrain on which all subsequent work in this book will operate. National identity is multiple, contested, and unevenly perceived. The Hexagon allows us to see its dimensions. The Country of Origin Effect reminds us that it is being transmitted constantly whether we act or not. The three-plane analysis shows us where our actual leverage lies. And the fact of plural identity prevents us from mistaking the convenience of a unified message for the truth of a unified country.

---

15. On the link between soft power and the attractiveness of pluralistic, democratic societies, see Nye's argument that soft power arises from the attractiveness of a country's culture, political ideals, and policies, as opposed to coercive hard power. Nye, Joseph S. *Soft Power: The Means to Success in World Politics*. PublicAffairs, 2004, ch. 1, pp. 1–32.

CHAPTER 3
SOFT POWER
ATTRACTION INSTEAD
OF COERCION

T here is a particular kind of power that leaves no fingerprints. It does not march across borders, does not freeze bank accounts, does not impose tariffs. It moves quietly, through films and universities, through the example of institutions that work, through the memory of a diplomat who listened more than she spoke. It is the power that makes a foreign student choose Heidelberg over its alternatives, that makes an entrepreneur in Lagos or São Paulo want to do business in Copenhagen, that makes a young filmmaker in Seoul confident that her story will travel. It is rarely announced, and when it is announced too loudly it tends to evaporate. For more than three decades, we have had a name for it: soft power.[1]

The concept is deceptively simple and, as we will see, considerably more difficult in practice than its first formulation suggests. *Attraction instead of coercion.* The capacity to shape what others want rather than to constrain what they do. That such a formulation should have become the

---

1. Joseph Nye coined the term «soft power» in his 1990 book *Bound to Lead*, which challenged the prevailing view of American decline by arguing that power also consists in the ability to affect others by attraction and persuasion rather than just coercion and payment. See Nye, Joseph S., Jr. *Bound to Lead: The Changing Nature of American Power*. Basic Books, 1990.

central lens through which governments, consultancies, academics, and communication professionals now think about international influence is itself a historical event – one that deserves to be examined before we begin using the concept as if it were a neutral descriptive tool. Soft power is not neutral. It is a theory, and like all theories it illuminates certain things and obscures others. This chapter traces its origin, maps its architecture, interrogates its paradoxes, and then turns to the harder question of how one measures a force that works best when it is not seen working.

3.1 THE CONCEPTUAL REVOLUTION

When Joseph Nye introduced the term «soft power» in the closing years of the Cold War,[2] the dominant framework for understanding international relations was *realism*, a tradition stretching from Thucydides through Hobbes to the twentieth-century theorists of the balance of power.[3] Realism taught that states were rational actors in an anarchical system, and that power could be inventoried: troop counts, nuclear warheads, gross domestic product, industrial capacity, naval tonnage. Influence was a function of material capability, and capability was, in principle, countable.

Nye's intervention was not to deny the relevance of these hard metrics. It was to argue that they were radically incomplete. A state could possess overwhelming military force and yet fail to achieve its strategic objectives because other states refused to cooperate, because populations rejected its legitimacy, because its behavior generated resistance rather than alignment. Conversely, a state with modest material resources could achieve disproportionate influence because other actors actively wanted what it represented – its culture, its institutions, its way of life. Power, Nye argued, was fundamentally relational and perceptual.[4] It was produced not

---

2. Nye first formulated the concept in his 1990 volume, writing that "when one country gets other countries to want what it wants might be called co-optive or soft power in contrast with the hard or command power of ordering others to do what it wants." Nye, Joseph S., Jr. *Bound to Lead: The Changing Nature of American Power*. Basic Books, 1990, p. 31.
3. For the canonical statement of neorealist theory against which Nye positioned his intervention, see Waltz, Kenneth N. *Theory of International Politics*. Addison-Wesley, 1979. Nye explicitly cites Waltz's work as the background reference for realist power theory.
4. Nye situates his soft-power framework within the lineage of what Peter Bachrach and

only in the capacity to constrain behavior but in the capacity to shape preferences.[5]

This was a quiet revolution. It reframed power as something that happened in the minds of others, which meant that the sites of power were no longer exclusively the ministry of defense and the treasury but also the university, the cinema, the news bureau, the cultural institute, the embassy. It suggested that a nation's foreign behavior, the quality of its domestic institutions, and the global circulation of its artistic and intellectual production were not peripheral to its strategic position but constitutive of it. And it offered something that traditional realism could not: a vocabulary for explaining why, despite their material might, certain powers had declined in global influence, and why certain small and medium states punched far above their weight.

The rapid adoption of soft power by policymakers is telling. It was seized upon not only because it was analytically useful but because it offered a rhetorical alternative to nations uncomfortable with or excluded from traditional hard-power competition. For mid-sized democracies, post-colonial states, and rising powers seeking a legitimate global profile, soft power promised a path to influence that did not require aircraft carriers. This is why the concept traveled so quickly across so many capitals, and why it has become, for better or worse, the default framework within which contemporary thinking about national image is conducted.

3.2 THE THREE PILLARS

Nye organized the sources of soft power into three categories that have since become the standard architecture of the field: culture, political

---

Morton Baratz (1962) called the "second face of power," a theoretical heritage he developed more fully in *Soft Power: The Means to Success in World Politics*. See Nye, Joseph S., Jr. "Public Diplomacy and Soft Power." *The Annals of the American Academy of Political and Social Science*, vol. 616, 2008, pp. 94–109.

5.   On the relational and perceptual nature of power, see Nye, Joseph S., Jr. *The Paradox of American Power: Why the World's Only Superpower Can't Go It Alone.* Oxford University Press, 2002. Here Nye argued that in the coming century the United States would rely less on military might and more on the power that derives from the appeal of its culture, values, and institutions.

values, and foreign policy.[6] Each is worth examining on its own terms before we consider how they interact.

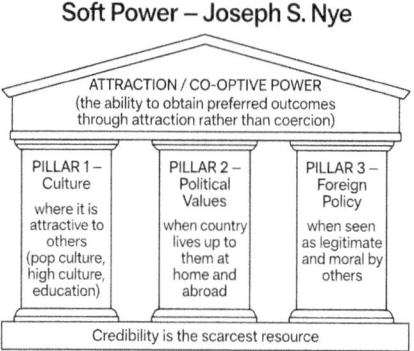

Fig. 3 - Nye's Three Pillars of Soft Power.

Culture produces soft power when it is attractive to others. The emphasis matters. A nation may possess an extraordinary cultural tradition and derive no soft power from it whatsoever if that tradition remains inaccessible, untranslated, or perceived as foreign in a negative sense. Culture becomes a source of attraction when it generates desire, admiration, curiosity, or identification across borders – when people elsewhere want to consume it, study it, imitate it, or travel to encounter it. This is why the most robust cultural soft power tends to combine high culture (literature, art, philosophy) with popular culture (cinema, music, cuisine, sport) and with what might be called everyday culture (design, fashion, hospitality, urban life). Each register reaches different audiences through different channels, but all three must be present and circulating for a cultural footprint to translate into influence.

Political values generate soft power when they are perceived as legitimate or worth emulating. Democracy, the rule of law, the protection of human rights, functioning public institutions, social cohesion, ecological responsibility – these are not universally attractive in the abstract, and the

6. Nye elaborated this tripartite architecture in his 2004 volume, where he argued that a country's soft power rests on the attractiveness of its culture, its political values, and its policies. Nye, Joseph S., Jr. *Soft Power: The Means to Success in World Politics.* PublicAffairs, 2004.

history of attempts to export political values is a history of resistance, backlash, and unintended consequences. But when a nation's institutions are seen to work, when its citizens are visibly free and relatively content, when its public sphere is credible, the example exerts a pull that no communication campaign can manufacture. The Scandinavian countries, for most of the last half century, have derived enormous soft power from precisely this pillar, with relatively little overt cultural projection.

Foreign policy contributes to soft power when it is perceived as principled and legitimate, even by actors who may disagree with specific decisions. The key word is *perceived*. A foreign policy can be strategically sound and still generate resentment if it is experienced abroad as arrogant or indifferent to the concerns of others. Conversely, a policy that aligns itself with broadly recognized principles – multilateralism, respect for sovereignty, and, where there is wide consensus, humanitarian action in cases of genuine need – accumulates credibility that can be drawn upon in later moments of crisis.

The three pillars reinforce each other when aligned. A nation with attractive cultural exports, credible domestic institutions, and a foreign policy perceived as principled generates a coherent and mutually amplifying signal. But they also undermine each other when they contradict. This is the crucial diagnostic point, and it is where many nation branding efforts fail. Cultural exports cannot compensate indefinitely for a foreign policy widely perceived as unjust. A sophisticated tourism campaign cannot offset the reputational damage[7] of a visible failure of domestic institutions. The three pillars are not a portfolio from which a communicator can select the strongest; they are an integrated system, and audiences read them as such.

---

7. G. John Ikenberry's review of Nye's work underscores this diagnostic point, observing that international publics may embrace a country's values and culture while resisting its foreign policies, demonstrating how contradictions among the three pillars undermine their mutual reinforcement. Ikenberry, G. John. Review of *Soft Power: The Means to Success in World Politics*, by Joseph S. Nye, Jr. *Foreign Affairs*, vol. 83, no. 3, 2004, pp. 136–37.

3.3 A DISTINCTION THAT IS NEVER CLEAN

It would be convenient, analytically, if soft and hard power occupied cleanly separable domains. They do not. In operational reality, nations deploy both simultaneously, and each tends to be used to enable the other. Military alliances create the conditions for cultural exchange; cultural familiarity lubricates economic cooperation; economic cooperation underwrites diplomatic capital. The categories are distinct in theory and entangled in practice.

The entanglement has become more complicated with the emergence of what analysts now call *sharp power*[8] – the use of informational manipulation, covert influence operations, digital disinformation, and strategic interference in the public spheres of other states. Sharp power is not soft, because it works through deception rather than attraction.[9] It is not quite hard, because it does not rely on physical or economic coercion. It occupies a hybrid space that has become increasingly consequential, and any honest treatment of soft power today must acknowledge that the informational environment through which attraction circulates has been significantly contaminated by actors pursuing influence through manipulation rather than appeal.

Economic power is particularly ambiguous. Sanctions coerce. Trade relationships attract. Foreign direct investment can be experienced either as a generous partnership or as a subtle form of dependency. The same underlying material capability – a large domestic market, a reserve currency, a dominant position in some strategic sector – can produce either

---

8. The term was popularized in a December 2017 report by the National Endowment for Democracy's International Forum for Democratic Studies, which argued that "we are in need of a new vocabulary to describe this phenomenon" and that authoritarian influence efforts "pierce, penetrate, or perforate the information environments in the targeted countries." Walker, Christopher, and Jessica Ludwig, editors. *Sharp Power: Rising Authoritarian Influence*. National Endowment for Democracy, December 2017.

9. Walker and Ludwig emphasize that interpreting authoritarian influence efforts as attempts to boost soft power "misses the mark," because such actors "are not engaged in a form of public diplomacy as democracies would understand it." Walker, Christopher, and Jessica Ludwig. "The Meaning of Sharp Power: How Authoritarian States Project Influence." *Foreign Affairs*, 16 Nov. 2017.

attraction or resentment depending on how it is wielded. This is why Nye himself, in later work, adopted and systematized the concept of *smart power*,[10] which simply acknowledges that soft and hard are tools in a single strategic repertoire rather than opposing categories or moral alternatives.

A last caveat is worth stating plainly: the distinction between soft and hard should be used diagnostically, not as a moral ranking. Soft power is not intrinsically virtuous.[11] A nation can derive attraction from its wealth, its exclusivity, its glamour, its capacity to dominate global entertainment – without any of these resting on what anyone would call ethical foundations. Hard power is not automatically cynical; the credible capacity to defend oneself or an ally is often a precondition for the political stability within which soft power can flourish. The communicator who treats soft power as morally superior misreads its nature and will, sooner or later, be surprised by the reality of how it actually operates.

3.4 THE PARADOX OF ATTRACTION

Here we arrive at the concept's most disconcerting feature, and the one that every communication professional working on national image must eventually confront. *Soft power is frequently most effective when it is not actively pursued.* Cultural, political, and ethical attractiveness tends to emerge organically from the life of a society – from its institutions, its creative ecosystems, its civic habits – rather than from deliberate strategy. And overt attempts to build soft power often produce the opposite of the intended effect. They appear propagandistic. They undermine the very

---

10. Although the term is widely attributed to Nye, scholarly reconstruction credits Suzanne Nossel, who published "Smart Power" in *Foreign Affairs* in 2004, with its first formulation; Nye subsequently adopted and systematized the concept. See Nossel, Suzanne. "Smart Power." *Foreign Affairs*, vol. 83, no. 2, 2004, pp. 131–42.

11. Jonathan McClory notes that soft power "is too often misappropriated to cover all courses of action outside military force and, as such, is often embraced as the ethical alternative," while emphasizing that soft power can be wielded for harmful as well as benign purposes. McClory, Jonathan. *The Soft Power 30: A Global Ranking of Soft Power*. Portland Communications, 2015.

credibility they are designed to establish. Audiences sense the effort, and effort, in the domain of attraction, is nearly always counterproductive.[12]

This observation is not speculative. It is borne out by the pattern of which countries actually score highest on international measures of attractiveness. A striking regularity emerges: many of the nations with the greatest soft power have the least elaborate, least visible, least centralized nation branding apparatus. Their attractiveness is produced, largely, by the ordinary functioning of their societies – by universities that work, cities that are livable, films that find foreign audiences, diplomats who keep their word – rather than by ministries of image management. Meanwhile, several of the countries that have invested most heavily and visibly in strategic communication have seen those investments yield disappointing and sometimes negative returns.

This suggests a structural ceiling on nation branding understood as pure technique. The more visible the effort to produce attraction, the weaker its actual effect on foreign audiences. The implication for communication professionals is sobering, and it is worth stating without softening: invisibility, authenticity, and restraint may matter more for durable attraction than sophisticated strategic messaging. This is not an argument against doing communication work; it is an argument for doing it with a precise understanding of what communication can and cannot accomplish, and for prioritizing long, quiet, substantive approaches over loud and campaign-driven ones.

3.5 COMMUNICATION AMPLIFIES BUT DOES NOT SUBSTITUTE

If we take the paradox of attraction seriously, the role of communication in soft power strategy must be understood with care. Communication can do real work. It can render existing soft power assets visible to audiences who

---

12. Nye argued that in the domain of soft power "the best propaganda is not propaganda," further explaining that in the Information Age "credibility is the scarcest resource," and warning that information that appears to be propaganda may not only be scorned but also prove counterproductive by undermining a country's reputation for credibility. Nye, Joseph S., Jr. *Soft Power: The Means to Success in World Politics*. PublicAffairs, 2004, p. 111.

would otherwise overlook them, miss them entirely, or misperceive them through outdated stereotypes. A country with extraordinary design traditions, world-class research institutions, or a strong ecological track record may receive almost no international recognition for these if nothing is done to make them legible beyond its borders. Communication, in this sense, is a precondition for attraction to circulate – not its source, but its vehicle.

What communication *cannot* do is generate soft power where substantive foundations are absent. No campaign produces cultural vitality from nothing, manufactures political legitimacy where institutions are hollow, or confers moral credibility on conduct that audiences can see contradicts the claims being made. This is not a theoretical limit; it is an empirical one, observable across decades of failed image campaigns whose sophistication could not compensate for the gap between the story being told and the reality being experienced by foreign publics.

The most productive role of communication in soft power strategy, then, is *translation*. Translation in the literal sense – making linguistic access possible – but also in the broader sense of rendering national realities legible to foreign audiences within their own frames of reference, their own concerns, their own aesthetic sensibilities. A nation's achievements and virtues do not travel on their own; they must be transposed, contextualized, narrativized. This is honest communication work, and it is indispensable. But when communication runs ahead of substance, it produces a form of reputational inflation that inevitably corrects itself through direct exposure and comparison with reality. The students arrive and find the university is not what the brochure promised. The investor encounters the institution and discovers the bureaucratic dysfunction that no campaign mentioned. Each such encounter erodes trust more than a hundred campaigns can rebuild it.

This principle reframes the communicator's role. Not as a creator of soft power but as its *curator*, its *translator*, and its *amplifier*. The distinction is not semantic. It determines what kinds of projects are worth funding, what kinds of claims are worth making, and what kinds of expectations a communication strategy can legitimately be asked to fulfill.

3.6 MEASURING THE IMMEASURABLE

Anything that matters strategically will eventually be asked to account for itself in numbers. Soft power is no exception, and it presents measurement with a particularly difficult problem. Its effects are indirect, delayed, and often counterfactual. A war avoided. A trade agreement facilitated. An investment attracted that might have gone elsewhere. A talented researcher who chose one country over another. None of these outcomes leave the sort of trace that lends itself readily to quantification. What would it mean to count the conflicts that did not occur because a nation was trusted?

The field has nonetheless developed instruments that attempt to convert perception into tractable numbers, and the most widely used is the *Anholt-Ipsos Nation Brands Index*.[13] Building on Simon Anholt's original *Hexagon* model – the six dimensions of exports, governance, culture, people, tourism, and investment and immigration[14] – the Index extends this framework into an annual global survey of international publics, producing a ranking of fifty nations across its six dimensions. Its value lies in a methodological consistency sustained over nearly two decades, which allows for the tracking of shifts in perception over time with a degree of reliability that isolated studies cannot match.

Yet any such instrument rests on methodological choices that determine what it sees. Which dimensions are included and which are left out. How the dimensions are weighted against one another. Which international publics are surveyed, in which countries, in what numbers. Which indicators within each dimension are treated as decisive. These choices are not arbitrary, but they are choices, and different indices – the

---

13. The Index is "based on the Hexagon of National Image, a model developed by Simon Anholt in the 1990s," whose six points constitute the "natural channels through which countries create their images." See Ipsos Public Affairs. *Anholt-Ipsos Nation Brands Index (NBI): Taking Your Reputation Places*. Ipsos, 2021.

14. The NBI polls roughly 40,000 people across 20 countries annually to gather insights about 50 countries based on global perceptions of six aspects of a nation's identity: exports, governance, culture, people, tourism, and investment potential, which together constitute the Nation Brand Hexagon. "Anholt Nation Brands Index (NBI) 2024: Key Highlights and Trends." *The Place Brand Observer*, 2025.

Portland Soft Power 30,[15] the *Brand Finance Global Soft Power Index*, and others[16] – make them differently. This is why the same country can rank differently across instruments. It is not that one index is right and another wrong; it is that they have operationalized «soft power» different-ly,[17] and each is seeing a slightly different object.

Anholt-Ipsos Nation Brands Index (NBI)
The measurement extension of the Nation Brand Hexagon

Fig. 4 - Anholt-Ipsos Nation Brands Index (NBI).

15. The Portland Soft Power 30 was launched by Portland Communications in 2015, and from the third edition (2017) onward has been produced in collaboration with the University of Southern California Center on Public Diplomacy. For the methodology, see McClory, Jonathan, and Olivia Harvey. "The Soft Power 30: Getting to Grips with the Measurement Challenge." *Global Affairs*, vol. 2, no. 3, 2016, pp. 309–19.

16. Brand Finance publishes the Index "based on a survey of more than 150,000 respondents from over 100 countries ranking global perceptions of all 193 member states of the United Nations," defining soft power as a nation's ability to influence the preferences and behaviors of other nations through attraction and persuasion rather than coercion. Brand Finance. *Global Soft Power Index 2026*. Brand Finance, 2026.

17. Cevik and Padilha note that the construction of any composite index depends critically on choices about how to weight its constituent variables, and that such weighting decisions, regardless of the technique adopted, ultimately reflect value judgments rather than purely technical determinations – a methodological caveat that undergirds the present chapter's argument about cross-index incommensurability. See Cevik, Serhan, and Tales Padilha. *Measuring Soft Power: A New Global Index*. IMF Working Paper No. 24/212, International Monetary Fund, October 2024.

The practical implication is that such instruments are most reliable as trackers of change within a single methodology over time, and less reliable as cross-index comparisons of absolute position. A country whose NBI rank has moved five places up or down has moved – something has shifted in the perceptions the Index is designed to capture. A country that ranks higher in one index than in another has been measured differently, and the gap tells us more about the instruments than about the country. Used this way, indices become genuinely useful diagnostic tools. Misused as absolute scoreboards, they generate more confusion than clarity.

The deeper honesty about measurement is that it is always partial. Indices see what their methodologies are designed to see; they miss what their methodologies are not designed to capture. They can tell us that a country's perceived governance has improved relative to its perceived culture. They cannot tell us why, nor what lies beneath the shift, nor whether the shift will persist. Using these instruments responsibly means holding their limits and their insights in the same hand – trusting them enough to track movement over time, distrusting them enough to keep asking what their numbers leave out.

CHAPTER 4
THE PERSISTENCE OF PERCEPTION
STEREOTYPES, IDENTITY, AND MENTAL IMAGES

There is a question that every minister of foreign affairs, every tourism director, and every nation branding consultant eventually asks[1], usually in a moment of frustration: why is it so hard to change what people think of our country? The budgets are spent, the campaigns are launched, the visiting journalists are impressed, the films are produced, the international awards are won, the exports are certified, and yet the old image persists. Germans remain efficient. Italians remain creative. The French remain charming. Africa remains, for far too many audiences, a country rather than a continent[2]. Latin America remains

---

1. The foundational figure of this field is Simon Anholt. See Simon Anholt, *Competitive Identity: The New Brand Management for Nations, Cities and Regions*, Palgrave Macmillan, 2007. In 2005, Simon Anholt launched the Nation Brands Index, the first systematic study of country images; the NBI now incorporates nearly one billion datapoints of world-class research data, updated annually. For Anholt's own skepticism about branding shortcuts, see his argument that practitioners should focus on development and policy rather than chase the chimera of branding, since only a consistent, coordinated, and unbroken stream of useful, noticeable, world-class, and above all relevant ideas, products, and policies can, gradually, enhance the reputation of a country. Simon Anholt, "Beyond the Nation Brand: The Role of Image and Identity in International Relations," *Exchange: The Journal of Public Diplomacy*, vol. 2, no. 1, 2013, pp. 6–12.
2. For a book-length corrective to this persistent misconception, see Dipo Faloyin, *Africa Is Not a Country: Breaking Stereotypes of Modern Africa*, Harvill Secker, 2022 (published in

picturesque. The United States remains powerful and organized. And Switzerland, whatever it does, remains Switzerland.

This stubbornness is not an accident. It is not the result of bad communication strategy, nor of insufficient investment, nor of cultural prejudice in the moral sense. It is the visible effect of something deeper: the cognitive, social, and semiotic architecture through which human beings process information about groups they do not know personally. National stereotypes are among the most stable features of international perception precisely because they are not, in the first instance, beliefs about countries. They are tools the human mind uses to make sense of a world that contains far more nations than any individual can meaningfully know.

This chapter advances a sobering but necessary argument. Most of what shapes a country's image is what we will call cognitive infrastructure: the mental structures through which audiences encode, store, and retrieve information about nations. And cognitive infrastructure does not update through advertising. It updates through the slow, uneven, accumulated experience of generations, through shifts in geopolitical position, through the gradual renegotiation of cultural meaning, and through events dramatic enough to break existing frames. Communication accompanies these shifts; it rarely causes them.

To understand why, and to understand what communication professionals working on national image can realistically do, we must look at four bodies of thought that together map the terrain: the social psychology of group identity developed by Henri Tajfel[3], the dramaturgical sociology

the United States as *Africa Is Not a Country: Notes on a Bright Continent*, W. W. Norton, 2022). Faloyin, a senior editor at Vice, lambasts colonialists, charities, and the media for flattening a continent of fifty-four countries into a single narrative; in the introduction, he writes, "Not everyone is allowed a complex identity," arguing that few entities have been forced through a field of distorted reality as many times as Africa. See also the "Africa Is Not a Country" campaign by the African Students Association of Ithaca College, documented in Teo Kermeliotis, "'Africa Is Not a Country': Campaign Dispels Stereotypes," *CNN*, 7 Feb. 2014, which describes "The Real Africa: Fight the Stereotype," a social media initiative that aims to raise awareness about common misunderstandings such as the idea of Africa as a homogeneous entity rather than a diverse continent of more than fifty countries.

3. Tajfel's biography is crucial for understanding the stakes of his work. Michael Billig has noted that in his minimal group studies, Tajfel – of Polish-Jewish background and a survivor of the Second World War who lost many family members and friends between 1939 and

of Erving Goffman[4], the cultural semiotics of Stuart Hall[5], and the contemporary Stereotype Content Model developed by Susan Fiske and her collaborators[6]. Each illuminates a different face of the same underlying phenomenon. Read together, they form a realistic working theory of national image – one that respects the limits of persuasion while clarifying the genuine room for maneuver that remains.

4.1 HOW A MENTAL IMAGE OF A COUNTRY FORMS

Ask an ordinary person in Buenos Aires what they associate with Norway, or an ordinary person in Seoul what they associate with Portugal, and you will rarely receive a detailed briefing. You will receive a handful of images: a fjord, a Viking, perhaps cold; port wine, football, Cristiano Ronaldo, perhaps the navigators of the fifteenth century. These are not the results of careful study. They are the residue of a lifetime of incidental

---

1945 – was investigating an underlying question: how is genocide possible? For a foundational text, see Henri Tajfel and John C. Turner, "An Integrative Theory of Intergroup Conflict," *The Social Psychology of Intergroup Relations*, edited by W. G. Austin and S. Worchel, Brooks/Cole, 1979, pp. 33–47.

4. See Erving Goffman, *The Presentation of Self in Everyday Life*, Doubleday Anchor, 1959. Originally published in Scotland in 1956 and in the United States in 1959, it is Goffman's first and most famous book, for which he received the American Sociological Association's MacIver award in 1961; in 1998, the International Sociological Association listed the work as the tenth most important sociological book of the twentieth century.

5. For Hall's foundational statement on representation, see Stuart Hall, editor, *Representation: Cultural Representations and Signifying Practices*, Sage Publications, 1997. Richard Hoggart founded the Centre for Contemporary Cultural Studies at the University of Birmingham in 1964; Hall joined the Centre at Hoggart's invitation and took over from Hoggart as acting director in 1968, becoming director in 1972 and remaining there until 1979. Together with Hoggart and Raymond Williams, Hall is widely considered one of the founding figures of British Cultural Studies as a discipline.

6. See Susan T. Fiske, Amy J. C. Cuddy, Peter Glick, and Jun Xu, "A Model of (Often Mixed) Stereotype Content: Competence and Warmth Respectively Follow from Perceived Status and Competition," *Journal of Personality and Social Psychology*, vol. 82, no. 6, 2002, pp. 878–902. The model proposes that two primary dimensions – warmth and competence – organize group perception, that frequent mixed clusters combine high warmth with low competence (paternalistic) or high competence with low warmth (envious), and that distinct emotions (pity, envy, admiration, contempt) differentiate the four warmth-competence combinations; in the model, status predicts perceived competence, and competition predicts low perceived warmth.

exposure: a childhood atlas, a school lesson, a film half-watched, a sports broadcast, a news headline, a migrant colleague, a consumer product whose origin was legible on the label.

This is how mental images of foreign countries form for the overwhelming majority of the world's population. Direct experience is rare; indirect exposure is continuous and cumulative. Media, fiction, education, consumer goods, sports, cuisine, and occasional encounters with nationals – these are the ordinary channels through which a country acquires its foreign face. The face is assembled not logically but associatively: country X becomes linked to a small, salient bundle of traits, events, places, and figures, and that bundle *becomes* the country for all practical cognitive purposes.

Three features of this process matter enormously for anyone working on national image. First, these mental images crystallize early in life. By late adolescence, most people have a working mental map of the world's major countries that will change only marginally for the rest of their lives, unless disrupted by significant personal events such as migration, professional specialization, or marriage across borders. Second, once formed, the image operates as a perceptual filter. New information about the country is not processed on its own terms; it is interpreted and remembered through the existing structure. Information that confirms the image is absorbed and strengthens it. Information that contradicts it is often discounted, forgotten, or reframed as an exception that proves the rule. Third, and most consequential, the image is remarkably robust to direct personal experience. A tourist who has a wonderful week in a country reputed to be dangerous typically returns home convinced that they were lucky, not that the reputation was wrong.

The practical implication is severe. National reputation is not built in campaigns; it is accumulated over generations, and it lives primarily in collective memory. A country that hopes to change its image in five years is working against the grain of human cognition. A country that works *with* the grain – that accepts the multi-decade horizon of reputation change and plans accordingly – has a chance. This is the first, and most often resisted, insight of professional national image work.

4.2 TAJFEL AND SOCIAL IDENTITY THEORY

If cognition explains why national images are stable, social psychology explains why they are rarely neutral. The most important framework here is the social identity theory developed by the Polish-British psychologist Henri Tajfel in the 1970s, in work shaped by his own experience of the Second World War. Tajfel's central insight, demonstrated in the now-classic minimal group paradigm experiments[7], was that human beings form group attachments and intergroup distinctions on the flimsiest of bases. Simply being told one belonged to the «red» group rather than the «blue» group – on criteria known to be arbitrary – was enough to generate systematic in-group favoritism and out-group differentiation. People allocated resources more generously to their own group, evaluated its members more positively, and perceived the other group as more homogeneous than their own[8].

Tajfel's conclusion was that these are not moral failures but cognitive mechanisms. Group membership contributes to self-concept[9]; maintaining a positive self-concept requires, in part, maintaining a positive distinction between one's own group and others. The mechanism runs quietly, beneath awareness, and it requires no hostility to operate.

---

7. The minimal group paradigm is a method employed in social psychology; experiments using this approach have shown that even arbitrary distinctions between groups – such as preferences for certain paintings or the color of assigned shirts – can trigger a tendency to favor one's own group at the expense of others, even when doing so means sacrificing in-group gain. The original source is Henri Tajfel, "Experiments in Intergroup Discrimination," *Scientific American*, vol. 223, no. 5, Nov. 1970, pp. 96–102.

8. This is the well-documented out-group homogeneity effect: members of in-groups tend to perceive members of their own group as more diverse than an out-group, and to perceive out-group members as more similar to one another – in shorthand, "they are alike; we are diverse." For the seminal empirical work, see Bernadette Park and Myron Rothbart, "Perception of Out-Group Homogeneity and Levels of Social Categorization: Memory for the Subordinate Attributes of In-Group and Out-Group Members," *Journal of Personality and Social Psychology*, vol. 42, no. 6, 1982, pp. 1051–1068.

9. A key assumption in social identity theory is that individuals are intrinsically motivated to achieve positive distinctiveness: they strive for a positive self-concept, and because individuals are partly defined and informed by their social identities, they also strive to achieve or maintain a positive social identity. See Henri Tajfel and John C. Turner, "An Integrative Theory of Intergroup Conflict," *The Social Psychology of Intergroup Relations*, edited by W. G. Austin and S. Worchel, Brooks/Cole, 1979, pp. 33–47.

National identity activates this mechanism at the largest scale available in ordinary social life. Compatriots become *us*; foreigners become *them*; the distinction becomes loaded with evaluative weight. This is why national stereotypes are rarely neutral descriptions. They tend to valorize the in-group and to simplify, and often devalue, the out-group – frequently in asymmetrical ways. A French observer and a German observer, looking at the same bilateral relationship, will tend to describe the other with different emphases, each shaped by the needs of their own national self-concept.

For a professional working on national image, the implication is structural. Every foreign audience perceives your country partly through the prism of its own identity. Your national image, in country A, is partly a function of how country A organizes itself, what it needs to valorize or differentiate itself against, what regional or historical tensions inhabit its public discourse. This means national image management is never a bilateral negotiation between a country and a monolithic foreign audience. It is a distributed conversation across dozens of national imaginaries, each with its own structural needs. The same facts about your country will be read differently in Mexico and in Mozambique not because of different information but because of different identities doing the reading. Strategies that ignore this structural asymmetry tend to produce messages that work in one market and backfire in another – a recurring frustration in global nation branding campaigns.

4.3 THE NATIONAL STEREOTYPE AS COGNITIVE STRUCTURE

National stereotypes, understood in this light, are not primarily errors. They are heuristics – cognitive shortcuts that reduce informational complexity in a world with nearly two hundred countries and far too little individual attention. They are efficient, widely shared, and functional even when inaccurate at the individual case level. The cognitive system resists updating a working shortcut unless confronted with strong, repeated, and salient counter-evidence. This resistance is not a flaw to be corrected; it is the feature that makes the shortcut useful in the first place.

The most robust contemporary map of stereotype structure is the Stereotype Content Model developed by the American social psychologist Susan Fiske and her collaborators beginning in the early 2000s. The model's claim, tested across many countries and many types of groups, is that group perceptions organize themselves along two fundamental dimensions: warmth (is this group benign or threatening toward us?) and competence (is this group capable or incompetent?). These two questions, Fiske argues, are the ones the cognitive system most urgently asks about any unfamiliar group, because they correspond to the two most consequential unknowns in any encounter: intention and capability[10].

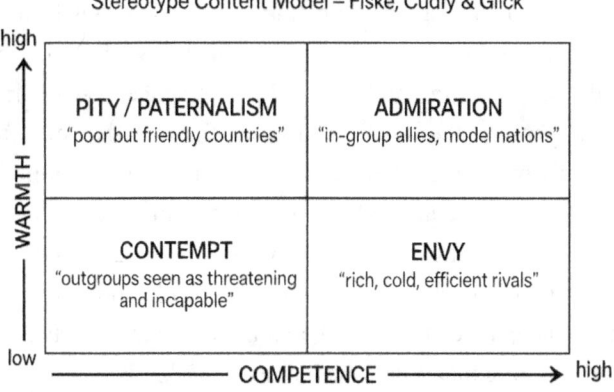

Fig. 5 - Stereotype Content Model (Fiske, Cuddy, Glick).

Applied to nations, the model reveals a stable pattern that any communication professional should know by heart. Countries are rarely perceived as high or low on both dimensions simultaneously. Most fall into mixed profiles, and each profile generates a distinctive emotional response. Countries perceived as high in both warmth and competence – typically

10. See Susan T. Fiske, "Stereotype Content: Warmth and Competence Endure," *Current Directions in Psychological Science*, vol. 27, no. 2, 2018, pp. 67–73. Humans are complicated stimuli, distinguished from most other objects by having intent and autonomy; people first want to know each other's individual or collective intent toward them and their groups, a dimension the SCM calls warmth (trustworthiness, sociability), which is fundamental because intent predicts behavior. Second, perceivers want to know whether others can enact that intent – how competent (capable, agentic) they are.

the in-group and close allies – elicit admiration. Countries perceived as high in competence but low in warmth – economic rivals, powerful former adversaries, nations whose efficiency or discipline is grudgingly acknowledged by neighboring regions – elicit envy and a grudging respect mixed with resentment[11]. Countries perceived as high in warmth but low in competence – small, sympathetic, economically weak nations – elicit a form of pity, a paternalistic affection[12] that is affectionate but diminishing. And countries perceived as low in both – typically those associated with poverty, conflict, and perceived dysfunction – elicit contempt, or at best indifference.

The practical consequences of this model are considerable. First, each quadrant has its own characteristic trap. High-competence, low-warmth countries that try to communicate greater capability reinforce the dimension that already feeds resentment. Low-competence, high-warmth countries that emphasize their charm deepen the paternalistic frame that prevents them from being taken seriously as economic or political actors. Second, the most consequential moves are usually cross-dimensional: a country perceived as efficient but cold needs to become warmer, not more efficient; a country perceived as charming but chaotic needs to demonstrate competence, not charm. Third, and most importantly, these shifts are slow. They require experiential evidence – new kinds of encounters, new categories of product, new roles in international crises – that displaces the existing position on one of the two axes. Communication can accompany this displacement; it cannot substitute for it.

---

11. Envious stereotypes attach to high-competence, low-warmth groups perceived to be doing better than others; this prediction receives support from findings that perceived power and status strongly predict perceived competence. See Fiske et al., "A Model of (Often Mixed) Stereotype Content," p. 881.

12. The second part of the social structure hypothesis holds that out-groups are seen as relatively warm and likable to the extent that they do not compete with the in-group. Compliant subordinate groups fulfill a convenient role and so receive paternalistic prejudice, which disrespects their competence but simultaneously approves of the qualities that keep them subordinate, so long as they pose no threat. See Fiske et al., "A Model of (Often Mixed) Stereotype Content," *Journal of Personality and Social Psychology*, vol. 82, no. 6, 2002, pp. 878–902.

4.4 GOFFMAN AND IMPRESSION MANAGEMENT

If Tajfel and Fiske explain why national images are as they are, Erving Goffman explains what countries try to do about it. The Canadian-American sociologist's dramaturgical theory, developed in *The Presentation of Self in Everyday Life* and subsequent works[13], treats social interaction as performance. Actors – individual or collective – manage impressions to shape the responses of their audiences, making strategic decisions about what to reveal, what to conceal, what to emphasize, and what to stage.

Applied to nations, the framework is immediately illuminating. Countries are actors on an international stage, managing impressions before multiple simultaneous audiences with conflicting expectations. A single state visit must play well to domestic voters, to the host country's public, to regional neighbors, to investors, and to diaspora communities. A pavilion at a world expo must attract tourists, impress potential business partners, reassure allies, and avoid offending rivals. A cultural season abroad must please sophisticated curators without alienating ordinary audiences. The art of diplomacy, narrowly conceived, has always been the art of managing these simultaneous performances.

Goffman's most productive distinction, for our purposes, is between front-stage and back-stage. The front stage is where the performance happens: official communications, state visits, ceremonies, press conferences, logos, campaigns, pavilions. The back stage is where reality lives: actual policies, internal political dynamics, corruption cases, bureaucratic decisions, the texture of ordinary life. Classical nation branding assumed a relatively stable separation between the two. One could manage the front

---

13. Believing that all participants in social interactions are engaged in practices to avoid being embarrassed or embarrassing others, Goffman developed his dramaturgical analysis, observing a connection between the kinds of acts people put on in their daily life and theatrical performances; in social interaction, as in theatrical performance, there is a front region where the performers are on stage in front of the audiences, where the positive aspects of self and desired impressions are highlighted, and a back region, where individuals can prepare for or set aside their role. See *The Presentation of Self in Everyday Life*, Doubleday Anchor, 1959. For further reading on Goffman's later work, see also *Stigma: Notes on the Management of Spoiled Identity*, Prentice-Hall, 1963, and *Frame Analysis: An Essay on the Organization of Experience*, Harper & Row, 1974.

stage with a reasonable expectation that back-stage messiness would remain backstage.

This assumption is now obsolete. Modern media – journalistic, activist, and above all digital – progressively erodes the separation. What was once back-stage becomes front-stage through investigative journalism, leaks, citizen video, and the ambient transparency of a world in which everyone carries a camera. A police officer mistreating a demonstrator in a regional city is now a news item in London and Tokyo within hours. A politician's private remark is now a diplomatic incident. A corporate environmental violation is now a national reputational event. The time between back-stage action and front-stage exposure has collapsed toward zero.

The implication for national image management is severe. Strategies premised on managing the front stage while back-stage reality drifts in another direction will fail, and will typically fail in ways that are themselves newsworthy and reputationally damaging. The only sustainable strategy in the connected era is what one might call integrated performance: an alignment of front-stage communication with back-stage reality, or a willingness to address back-stage reality as part of front-stage communication. Countries that attempt to communicate a modern, open image while maintaining closed, opaque institutional realities are increasingly caught in the contradiction, often dramatically. Goffman, writing in the 1950s about waiters and surgeons, could not have anticipated this. But his framework, applied to the current media environment, delivers the diagnosis with precision.

4.5 STUART HALL AND THE POLITICS OF REPRESENTATION

There is a further layer that neither social psychology nor dramaturgical sociology fully captures, and for it we turn to the Jamaican-British cultural theorist Stuart Hall. Hall's central argument, developed across decades of work on media and representation, is that representation is not a neutral mirror of reality. It is a productive practice. Images of a country do not simply reflect the country; they construct it in the minds of audiences, and through that construction they shape the political, economic, and cultural possibilities available to it.

Who produces the image therefore matters decisively. Representations of nations are shaped by those with media power, not by the subjects being represented. Historically, representations of non-Western countries have been produced largely by Western media: their journalists, their film industries, their publishing houses, their platforms. This produces deep asymmetries of visibility, voice, and narrative authority that no communication campaign, however well funded, can correct on its own. A country can produce beautiful images of itself; it cannot straightforwardly cause those images to circulate at the scale, and with the authority, that other images already enjoy.

Hall's encoding/decoding model adds a second structural complication[14]. The meaning an audience takes from an image is not determined by the intention of the producer. Audiences decode messages through their own cultural codes, and these codes vary across regions, classes, generations, and political orientations. A tourism campaign celebrating a country's indigenous heritage may be decoded as «authenticity» by one audience and as «primitivism» by another. A campaign celebrating modernity may be decoded as «sophistication» by one audience and as «soulless imitation» by another. Strategic control over meaning is therefore structurally limited, not because strategists are incompetent, but because meaning lives in the audience, not in the message.

The politics of representation reframes national image management as partly a structural question, not a tactical one. Tactical questions – which message, which channel, which ambassador – operate within a field whose basic shape is determined by who controls the means of representation at global scale. A realistic national image strategy acknowledges this field,

---

14. Hall's model reframes the traditional linear sender-receiver model. Originally formulated for a 1973 conference of mass communications scholars and circulated as a Centre for Contemporary Cultural Studies stencilled paper, Hall's "Encoding and Decoding in the Television Discourse" offered a theoretical approach to how media messages are produced, disseminated, and interpreted, proposing that audience members play an active role in decoding messages, drawing on their own social contexts. See Stuart Hall, "Encoding/Decoding," *Culture, Media, Language*, edited by Stuart Hall et al., Hutchinson, 1980, pp. 128–138.

works within it where necessary, and seeks, where possible, to change it: by building domestic media capacity with international reach, by investing in cultural industries that travel, by cultivating relationships with international correspondents and platforms, and by empowering diaspora voices that can speak from within foreign publics rather than to them from outside.

4.6 WHAT COMMUNICATION CAN AND CANNOT CHANGE

It is time to state plainly what this combined framework implies for professional practice. The persistence of perception is not an obstacle to be overcome; it is a condition to be worked within. Communication has real power, but its power has a shape, and mistaking that shape is the source of most wasted national image budgets.

Communication can introduce new associations, making a country visible along dimensions where it had previously been absent from the international imagination. A country can reposition itself as a hub of tech-nological innovation, as South Korea has done with its tech and cultural industries. This is real work, and it is worth doing.

Communication can also refresh and reshape existing stereotypes, shifting their salience or valence, particularly when aligned with observ-able change in the country itself. The shift from Spain-as-bullfighting to Spain-as-gastronomy-and-design over a generation was not a pure communication achievement; it rested on actual transformations in Spanish cuisine, architecture, cinema, and civic life. But communication accompanied and amplified those transformations, and without it they would have traveled less far and less fast.

Communication cannot, however, erase entrenched negative associa-tions through repetition alone. Sustained counter-communication in the absence of underlying change often strengthens the stereotype it seeks to dismantle, by keeping it salient in public discourse and by triggering the cognitive phenomenon in which denials and corrections can paradoxically reinforce the original claim[15]. «We are not corrupt» keeps corruption in the

---

15. This phenomenon is often called the "backfire effect," though the empirical literature is

conversation. «We are not dangerous» keeps danger in the conversation. Silence on the stereotype, combined with visible action that makes it progressively less plausible, is almost always more effective than rhetorical confrontation.

The boundary between what communication can and cannot do is ultimately set by the depth, coherence, and emotional weight of the existing image in the target audience, and by the degree to which observable reality supports or contradicts the proposed new image. An honest professional assessment – the kind of assessment this book will insist on throughout – distinguishes what is open to persuasion from what is structural. The first is a communication task. The second requires policy, institutional reform, economic transformation, and time. Treating structural problems as communication problems wastes resources and erodes credibility. Treating communication problems as structural ones surrenders a genuine instrument of influence.

---

now contested. See Brendan Nyhan, "Why the Backfire Effect Does Not Explain the Durability of Political Misperceptions," *Proceedings of the National Academy of Sciences*, vol. 118, no. 15, 2021, e1912440117. Nyhan argues that the accuracy-increasing effects of corrective information like fact checks often do not last or accumulate; instead, they frequently seem to decay or be overwhelmed by cues from elites and the media promoting more congenial but less accurate claims, with the result that misperceptions typically persist in public opinion for years after they have been debunked. Memory dynamics also play a role: corrections can leave the original association more vivid than the denial, so that repeated rebuttal sometimes reinforces the very claim it seeks to dismantle.

CHAPTER 5
PUBLIC RELATIONS AND NATIONS
A POSSIBLE TOOL FOR AN IMPOSSIBLE CLIENT

T here is a professional truth that every communications practitioner who has ever worked on behalf of a government eventually discovers: the discipline of public relations was not built for this. It was built for companies with a CEO, for brands with a board, for organizations that could, if pressed, be persuaded to speak with a single voice. A nation cannot.

A nation is not a client in any sense that the founders of modern public relations would have recognized. It has no chief executive who can sign off on a message architecture, no legal department that can approve a crisis protocol, no marketing director who can centralize tone of voice across territories. It has presidents who inevitably contradict foreign ministers, ministries that compete with one another for the spotlight, opposition parties whose professional function is to undermine the government's preferred narrative, citizens who post what they please, and a diaspora that speaks in its own name from a thousand addresses. And yet the tools of public relations – the research, the planning, the messaging, the measurement, the crisis protocols – remain the most sophisticated body of applied knowledge humanity has developed for shaping how one entity is perceived by another. The question is not whether these tools apply to nations. They do. The question is how they must be adapted when the client is, in the most literal professional sense, impossible.

This chapter introduces three reference points drawn from the discipline's most mature body of thought. The first is James Grunig's Four Models of Public Relations, which remains the clearest map the field has produced of its own evolution, from crude publicity to genuine dialogue. The second is the Barcelona Principles, the international consensus on how communications impact should actually be measured – a consensus that has important things to say about the seductive temptation to count press releases rather than changed minds. The third is Timothy Coombs's Situational Crisis Communication Theory, which provides the most systematic framework available for thinking about what to say, and what not to say, when reputation is under sudden attack. Each of these frameworks was developed in the corporate world. Each breaks in interesting ways when stretched to fit a nation. And each breaks in ways that are themselves instructive: the points at which PR methodology buckles under the weight of national reputation are precisely the points at which the real work of country branding begins.

5.1 THE ORIGINS AND EVOLUTION OF A DISCIPLINE

Modern public relations is a twentieth-century invention, born at the intersection of four forces: the rise of mass-circulation journalism, the wartime information campaigns of the First World War[1], the expansion of American corporate capitalism, and the emerging social sciences of psychology and sociology. It is no accident that its two foundational figures, Ivy Lee and Edward Bernays, emerged from this environment. Lee[2], a former reporter, advised the Rockefellers to replace silence and evasion with

---

1. The Committee on Public Information (1917–1919), also known as the CPI or the Creel Committee, was an independent U.S. government agency designed to generate public support at home and overseas for America's involvement in the war.
2. Ivy Ledbetter Lee (July 16, 1877 – November 9, 1934) was an American publicity expert and a founder of modern public relations, best known for his public relations work with the Rockefeller family.

proactive communication after the Ludlow Massacre[3], pioneering the now-standard idea that a corporation under attack is better off telling its own story than letting others tell it – though the nature and accuracy of that storytelling would itself become an early subject of professional controversy. Bernays, Sigmund Freud's nephew[4], went further, arguing that public opinion could be systematically engineered through the application of psychological insight – an ambition he laid out with unsettling candor[5] in *Crystallizing Public Opinion* (1923) and, even more explicitly, in *Propaganda* (1928).[6] Between them, these two men set the polarities within which the profession still operates: honest disclosure on one end, strategic persuasion on the other, both of them deploying the growing sophistication of the social sciences in service of organizational objectives.

For most of the twentieth century, the field grew faster than it theorized itself. That changed with James Grunig, whose Excellence Study, conducted through the 1980s and early 1990s with the International Association of Business Communicators[7], produced what remains the most widely taught map of the discipline: the Four Models of Public Relations[8].

---

3. John D. Rockefeller Jr. brought in pioneer public relations expert Ivy Lee, who warned that the Rockefellers were losing public support and developed a strategy that Rockefeller followed to repair it, including going to Colorado personally to meet the miners and their families.

4. Bernays was a year old when his parents moved to New York City from Austria; his mother was Sigmund Freud's sister, Anna, and his father was a successful grain merchant. See Britannica, T. Editors of Encyclopaedia. "Edward Bernays." *Encyclopædia Britannica*, 5 Mar. 2026.

5. Edward Bernays worked on propaganda for the U.S. government during World War I, an experience that sparked his interest in the power of communication and persuasion; recognizing the negative connotation of "propaganda," he later redefined it as "public relations," emphasizing the psychological aspects of influencing public opinion. See Bernays, Edward L. *Propaganda*. Horace Liveright, 1928.

6. Of Bernays's many books, *Crystallizing Public Opinion* (1923) and *Propaganda* (1928) gained special attention as early efforts to define and theorize the field of public relations; citing works of writers such as Gustave Le Bon, Wilfred Trotter, Walter Lippmann, and Sigmund Freud, he described the masses as irrational.

7. The Excellence Study was funded by the IABC Research Foundation and headed by James E. Grunig of the University of Maryland, producing several volumes including *Excellence in Public Relations and Communication Management* (1992) and *Excellent Public Relations and Effective Organizations* (2002). See Grunig, James E., editor. *Excellence in Public Relations and Communication Management*. Lawrence Erlbaum Associates, 1992.

8. In their seminal work *Managing Public Relations*, James Grunig and Todd Hunt (1984)

Grunig's taxonomy is at once historical, practical, and quietly normative. It identifies four distinct ways organizations communicate with their publics, and invites practitioners to notice, honestly, which one they are actually doing.

Grunig & Hunt – Four Models of Public Relations

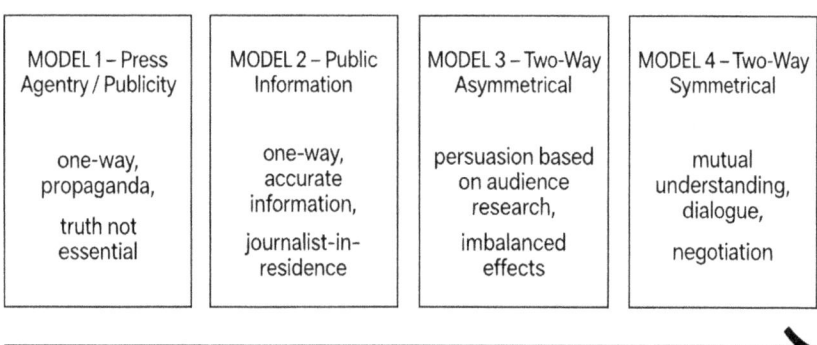

MODEL 1 – Press Agentry / Publicity	MODEL 2 – Public Information	MODEL 3 – Two-Way Asymmetrical	MODEL 4 – Two-Way Symmetrical
one-way, propaganda, truth not essential	one-way, accurate information, journalist-in-residence	persuasion based on audience research, imbalanced effects	mutual understanding, dialogue, negotiation

Fig. 6 - Grunig's Four Models of Public Relations.

The first model is *press agentry*, or publicity at any cost[9]. It is the oldest form, built around the conviction that attention itself is the goal and that accuracy is a secondary consideration at best. The second is the *public information model*, in which the organization takes on the role of a kind of in-house journalist, disseminating accurate, factual information in one direction to its audiences, without particular concern for what they think back. The third is *two-way asymmetric communication*, in which the organization listens to its audiences – through surveys, focus groups, analytics – but uses what it learns primarily to refine its own persuasion. The audience is researched so that the audience can be moved. The fourth is *two-*

---

introduced four models of public relations — press agentry, public information, two-way asymmetrical, and two-way symmetrical — that have since become the most widely cited in academic circles. See Grunig, James E., and Todd Hunt. *Managing Public Relations.* Holt, Rinehart and Winston, 1984.

9. Excellence Theory expands on four foundational PR models: the press agentry/publicity model, which focuses on persuasion and media attention, and the public information model, which emphasizes one-way dissemination of accurate information. See "Excellence Theory Explained (Core Concepts + Applications)." *The Commspot,* 24 Oct. 2025.

way symmetric communication, Grunig's ideal type[10], in which both organization and public adjust in response to dialogue. The organization is prepared to change, not merely to be more effectively persuasive.

Grunig did not claim that the later models had replaced the earlier ones. All four remain in daily use. A tourist board running a Times Square stunt is practicing press agentry. A central bank publishing quarterly statistics is practicing public information. A political campaign polling battleground districts to refine its message is engaged in two-way asymmetric communication. A government genuinely consulting its diaspora on visa reform and adjusting policy in response is engaged – rarely, imperfectly – in something approaching two-way symmetric practice.

The value of Grunig's framework for our purposes is *diagnostic* rather than *prescriptive*. It gives us a vocabulary for asking a question that most nations prefer not to answer: which kind of public relations is the state actually practicing, as distinct from which kind it claims to practice? Most national communication efforts are asymmetric at best, even when their official self-descriptions borrow the language of «dialogue» and «partnership». Recognizing this honestly is the first step toward doing the work better. The nations that most effectively build their international image over time tend to be those that have moved, at least in some domains, toward the symmetric end of the scale – not because symmetry is morally superior, but because in a networked information environment the asymmetric approach is increasingly visible as such, and increasingly discounted accordingly.

5.2 THE METHODOLOGICAL CORE

Strip away the jargon and the methodology of contemporary public relations reduces to a cycle of four stages: *research, strategy, execution, and measurement*. This is the operating logic inherited by every serious

---

10. According to Grunig and his team, excellent public relations programs share qualities including a strategic management function, empowered leadership, and symmetrical communication, which emphasizes dialogue, feedback, and collaboration over manipulation.

national communications program, and it is worth walking through it in terms specific to the reputation of a country.

- *Research* is where it begins, and where most national efforts are weakest. Sound practice requires understanding the perceptions that already exist among target audiences, the narratives currently circulating about the country in international media, the competitive communication environment – which other countries are crowding the same mental space, with what positioning – and the behavioral patterns of the audiences one hopes to reach. A Ministry of Tourism that commissions a campaign without first knowing what foreign travelers already believe about the country, what they fear, what they misremember, and what they confuse with the country next door, is operating in darkness. The research stage is also where the hardest intellectual work of country communication takes place, because research reveals the gap between how a nation sees itself and how others see it. That gap is often uncomfortable, and the temptation to skip past it toward execution is enormous.
- *Strategy* translates research into intent. It defines objectives in measurable terms, prioritizes audiences (because no nation has the resources to talk effectively to everyone), establishes a strategic position in relation to competitors, and builds a message architecture aligned with organizational reality. The last phrase matters. A national message architecture cannot be wishful. If the country aims to position itself as a «technology hub» but its broadband penetration is in the bottom quartile of its region, the position will collapse on first contact with a journalist who bothers to check. Strategy must be honest about what the country is, or at least what it is credibly becoming.
- *Execution* – message development and channel selection – converts strategy into concrete content placed where target audiences actually are. This is the stage at which the amateur and the professional diverge most visibly. The amateur selects

channels because they are available, familiar, or politically safe. The professional selects channels because they are where the target audience lives. German business press, Brazilian Instagram, Indonesian TikTok, Nigerian WhatsApp groups: these are not interchangeable, and neither are their audiences' standards of credibility.

- *Measurement* closes the loop, and this is where the international consensus in the form of the Barcelona Principles does its most useful work. First developed in 2010 by a group convened by the International Association for the Measurement and Evaluation of Communication (AMEC)[11], and now in their fourth edition[12], the Principles establish what good measurement actually looks like. Two of them are particularly relevant to national reputation work. The first is the insistence that measurement focus on outcomes and impact – changes in perception, attitude, and behavior – rather than outputs[13], which is to say press releases issued, events held, mentions generated. The second is the explicit rejection of Advertising Value Equivalent (AVE)[14], a discredited metric that counts a piece of editorial coverage as if it were equivalent to paid advertising of the same space, ignoring entirely the question of

---

11. The Barcelona Principles were agreed upon by PR practitioners from 33 countries who met in Barcelona, Spain in 2010 for a summit convened by the International Association for Measurement and Evaluation of Communication (AMEC); they identify the need for outcome-based, instead of output-based, measurement of PR campaigns and call for the exclusion of ad value equivalency metrics.

12. The Barcelona Principles 4.0 represent the fourth iteration of one of AMEC's flagship assets, launched in 2025. See "Introducing the AMEC Barcelona Principles 4.0: A New Era in PR Measurement." *AMEC*, 9 July 2025.

13. Outcomes include shifts in awareness, comprehension, attitude, and behavior related to purchase, donations, brand equity, corporate reputation, employee engagement, public policy, investment decisions, and other shifts in stakeholders regarding a company, NGO, government, or entity. See "Barcelona Declaration of Measurement Principles." *AMEC*, 19 July 2010.

14. Advertising Value Equivalents do not measure the value of public relations and do not inform future activity; they measure the cost of media space and are rejected as a concept to value public relations. See "Barcelona Declaration of Measurement Principles." *AMEC*, 19 July 2010.

whether the coverage was favorable, whether it reached the right audience, or whether it changed anything at all.

The Barcelona standard matters enormously for national reputation because the temptation at the national level is precisely to substitute outputs for outcomes. Press releases issued, state visits conducted, interviews granted, mentions generated: all of these can be counted, reported upwards, and entered into annual reviews. Whether the country is actually better understood, more respected, or more trusted than it was the year before is a harder question, which is why it is so often not asked. The discipline the Barcelona Principles impose – «measure what you actually want to change, not what is easiest to tally» – is the discipline most national communication programs most need and most often lack.

Barcelona Principles 3.0 (AMEC, 2020)

The international standard for measuring communication effects

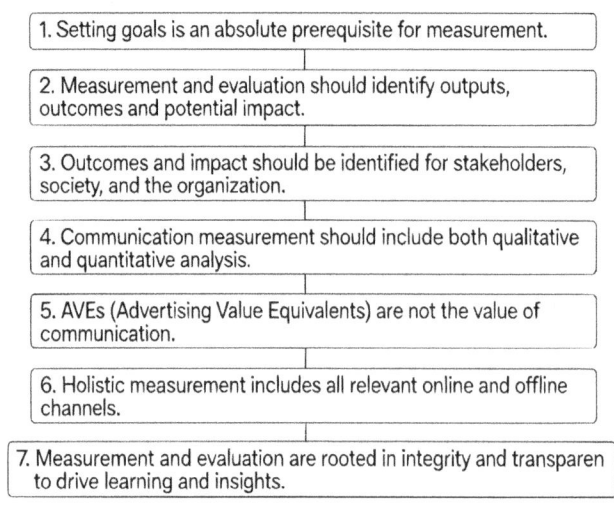

Fig. 7 - Barcelona Principles 3.0.

5.3 FROM CORPORATE CLIENT TO NATION-CLIENT

The methodology survives the leap from corporate to national scale. What changes is everything around it.

The first change is *the principal*. A corporation has a CEO. A nation does not. Authority over national communication is distributed across institutions – the presidency, the foreign ministry, the trade ministry, the tourism board, the central bank, the embassies – and contested between them, often with open hostility. Each institution has its own budget, its own stakeholders, its own political sponsors, and its own definition of success. There is no desk at which a national communications strategy can be approved and enforced across the whole apparatus. The implication for PR practice is that the national communicator spends a substantial portion of their time negotiating with their own side, and that *internal alignment is a precondition for external coherence*, not a given.

The second change is *the scale and diversity of stakeholders*. A corporation has customers, shareholders, employees, regulators, and perhaps a few adjacent publics. A nation has citizens, diaspora communities, foreign governments, international media, foreign investors, tourists, international NGOs, multilateral institutions, and supranational bodies. These publics pursue conflicting interests. The diaspora wants recognition and rights; foreign investors want predictability and low taxation; tourists want authenticity and safety; international media want stories and access; domestic citizens want sovereignty and economic improvement. No single message reaches all of them effectively, and indeed a message calibrated for one will often alienate another.

The third change is *time*. Corporate reputation can move in months; a well-executed rebrand, a successful product launch, or a well-handled crisis can shift perception within a single news cycle. National reputation shifts across decades. The international images that countries like Germany, Japan, South Korea, Ireland, and Rwanda enjoy today are the product of deliberate, patient work[15] that began, in most cases, decades

---

15. A recent study examines how nation branding driven by culture and heritage influences Rwanda's sustainable development, drawing on national identity and nation branding theo-

ago. Each of these nations faced distinct reputational challenges rooted in history, and each responded with sustained, long-term strategies of transformation and communication. Shorter horizons do not produce national reputation; they produce *campaigns*, which is a very different thing.

The fourth change is *control*. A corporation controls its products, its pricing, its packaging, its employees, and most of its public-facing communication. A nation controls almost none of its reputation directly. The country's reputation is produced by the collective output of millions of citizens, most of whom have no interest in image management, plus the coverage of a global press that owes the government nothing, plus the verdicts of international institutions that assess the country's performance on a dozen different dimensions, plus the experiences of every tourist, investor, and diplomat who interacts with the country at any level. The national communicator is not managing a reputation; they are *curating conditions under which a reputation can form*.

The implication is not that PR methodology should be abandoned. The implication is that it must be adapted, its expectations moderated, its horizons extended, and its practitioners resigned to a degree of humility that the corporate world does not require. The *listen-plan-communicate-measure* cycle still applies. It just operates across longer time spans, with more fragmented authority, and with far less control over outcomes.

5.4 STAKEHOLDER MAPPING WITHOUT A CENTER

Because no single message works for all national audiences, the *stakeholder map* becomes the organizing document of national PR practice. The discipline of mapping, borrowed from the corporate world, must be expanded considerably.

Stakeholders at the national level do not sit on a single plane. They operate in different roles simultaneously. International media are *amplifiers* – they rarely change behavior on their own but determine which

---

ries, and argues that cultural heritage is key to redefining Rwanda after the 1994 genocide against the Tutsi. See Muvunyi, Faustin, et al. "Cultural Heritage-Driven Nation Branding and Sustainable Development: Rebuilding National Identity in Rwanda." *African Journal of Empirical Research*, vol. 7, no. 1, 2026, pp. 1159–1173.

stories reach which audiences. Domestic citizens are *constituencies* – their support legitimizes the government that speaks in the nation's name, and their conduct shapes the country's image whether they intend to or not. Foreign investors are *clients in the commercial sense* – they make decisions based on assessed risk and return, and their decisions are themselves perception-shaping signals. Foreign governments function as *gatekeepers* – their recognition, sanction, or endorsement opens or closes doors. Diaspora communities are *proxies* – they represent the country in every society where they live, often more consistently than any embassy. International NGOs and multilateral institutions are *auditors*, issuing reports and rankings that become shorthand for the country's standing.

No single channel strategy reaches all of these effectively. A country that communicates with its diaspora through the same register it uses for international investors will fail with both. Stakeholder mapping therefore drives *message differentiation*, not message unification. The search for a single, universal national message is a mistake; what the country needs is a *stable core identity* from which differentiated messages can be credibly generated for specific audiences. The core must be consistent; the surface must adapt.

5.5 AGENDA SETTING AND FRAMING

Agenda-setting theory, developed by McCombs and Shaw in the 1970s[16], holds that while the media may not tell people what to think, they are remarkably effective at telling people what to think about[17]. For nations, this is the single most consequential communication dynamic at work. A country that can place itself on the international agenda for positive

---

16. McCombs and Shaw's seminal study on the agenda-setting function of mass media appeared in *Public Opinion Quarterly*, vol. 36, no. 2, Summer 1972, pp. 176–187. See McCombs, Maxwell E., and Donald L. Shaw. "The Agenda-Setting Function of Mass Media." *Public Opinion Quarterly*, vol. 36, no. 2, 1972, pp. 176–187.

17. Bernard Cohen (1963) refined Lippmann's ideas by pointing out that the media do not tell people what to think, but what to think about; Maxwell McCombs and Donald Shaw (1972) first put this idea to empirical test by comparing the news media agenda and the public agenda during the 1968 U.S. presidential election. See Cohen, Bernard C. *The Press and Foreign Policy*. Princeton UP, 1963.

reasons gains reputational ground almost automatically. A country absent from the international agenda entirely is effectively invisible, and *invisibility in the global conversation is itself a kind of slow reputational death*.

Framing is the second-order battle[18]. Once an event involving the country is on the agenda, the fight moves to the question of what it means. The same fact – a protest, an election, a recession, a natural disaster – can be framed as «resilience» or «fragility», as «recovery» or «decline», as evidence of «democracy working» or of «institutions failing». Nations that have invested in *narrative infrastructure* – credible spokespeople, trusted journalists who understand the country, well-briefed diplomats, sophisticated cultural institutions abroad – win framing battles more often. Nations that have not invested in this infrastructure have their framing done for them by others.

The long-term work of national public relations is therefore the patient construction of *agenda-setting and framing capacity*. The temptation to fight individual news cycles reactively is strong and almost always a mistake. The cycle will move on; the capacity, if built, will still be there next time.

5.6 CRISIS COMMUNICATION AT THE NATIONAL SCALE

Eventually every nation faces a reputational crisis: a scandal, a disaster, a diplomatic incident, a wave of protest, a collapse of some institution that the outside world was watching. These events can undo decades of patient image-building within weeks if handled badly. The most systematic framework for thinking about response is Timothy Coombs's Situational Crisis Communication Theory[19], which insists that *there is no single correct way*

---

18. To frame is to select some aspects of a perceived reality and make them more salient in a communicating text, in such a way as to promote a particular problem definition, causal interpretation, moral evaluation, and/or treatment recommendation for the item described. See Entman, Robert M. "Framing: Toward Clarification of a Fractured Paradigm." *Journal of Communication*, vol. 43, no. 4, 1993, pp. 51–58.

19. Situational Crisis Communication Theory was developed by W. Timothy Coombs, a communication scholar, building on attribution theory, which explores how people interpret the causes of events — especially negative ones — and assign responsibility. See Coombs, W. Timothy. "Protecting Organization Reputations During a Crisis: The Development and

to handle a crisis – the appropriate response depends on what kind of crisis it is.

SCCT – Situational Crisis Communication Theory (Coombs)

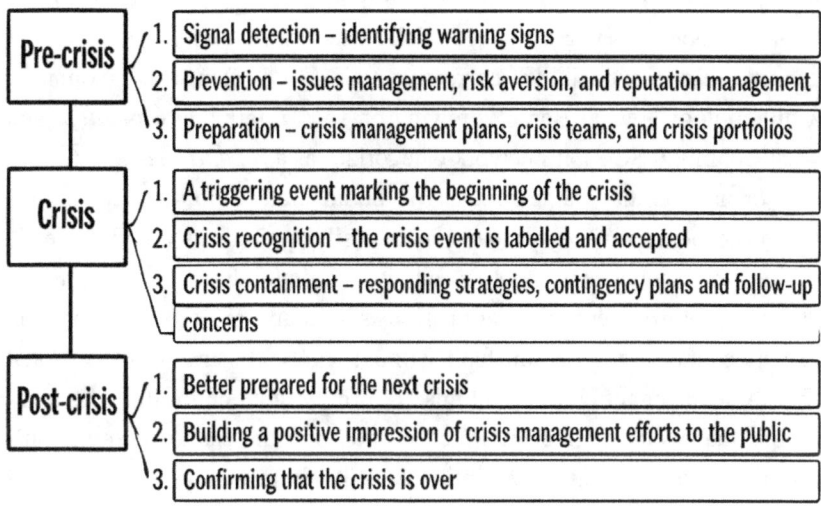

Pre-crisis	1.	Signal detection – identifying warning signs
	2.	Prevention – issues management, risk aversion, and reputation management
	3.	Preparation – crisis management plans, crisis teams, and crisis portfolios
Crisis	1.	A triggering event marking the beginning of the crisis
	2.	Crisis recognition – the crisis event is labelled and accepted
	3.	Crisis containment – responding strategies, contingency plans and follow-up concerns
Post-crisis	1.	Better prepared for the next crisis
	2.	Building a positive impression of crisis management efforts to the public
	3.	Confirming that the crisis is over

Fig. 8 - Situational Crisis Communication Theory (Coombs).

Coombs distinguishes three broad clusters[20]. *Victim crises* are those in which the organization is itself the victim[21]: natural disasters, external attacks, rumors spread by malicious actors. The appropriate response

---

Application of Situational Crisis Communication Theory." *Corporate Reputation Review*, vol. 10, no. 3, 2007, pp. 163–176.

20. SCCT divides crisis types into three crisis clusters: the victim cluster, defined as crises with weak attributions of organizational responsibility; the accidental cluster, in which a certain but low level of responsibility is attributed to the organization; and the preventable cluster, which includes crises for which the organization is perceived as being responsible. See Coombs, W. Timothy, and Sherry J. Holladay. "Helping Crisis Managers Protect Reputational Assets: Initial Tests of the Situational Crisis Communication Theory." *Management Communication Quarterly*, vol. 16, no. 2, 2002, pp. 165–186.

21. Victim crises (e.g., natural disasters, product tampering) involve little to no fault by the organization; accidental crises (e.g., technical failures, unintentional mistakes) imply limited responsibility; preventable crises (e.g., misconduct, negligence) place full responsibility on the organization. See "Situational Crisis Communication Theory (SCCT) Explained." *Anderson Executive Education*, 6 Nov. 2025.

emphasizes expressions of concern, provision of accurate information, and visible competence in response. *Accidental crises* are those caused by the organization but without malicious intent: technical failures, unintended harms, accidents. These require acknowledgment, explanation, and credible corrective action. *Preventable crises* are those caused by organizational misconduct, negligence, or deliberate wrongdoing. These require acceptance of responsibility, corrective action, and often what amounts to a full apology – what Benoit, drawing on Burke, terms *mortification* and what Coombs's SCCT framework categorizes as a *rebuild strategy*.[22]

For nations, the framework has to be adapted to political constraints that no corporation faces. A state cannot easily apologize without domestic political consequences – apology admits wrongdoing, and in a polarized domestic environment every admission is ammunition for the opposition. A state cannot always admit fault without legal exposure in international fora. A state cannot credibly promise reform without controlling the institutions that would deliver it, which is often not the case. And a nation's crisis response is itself a live political battle, fought between government and opposition in full view of the audience whose perceptions the crisis is already threatening.

The deeper lesson of Coombs's theory is *preparatory, not reactive.* The most damaging crises are those that confirm pre-existing negative stereotypes about the country; the least damaging are those that contradict them. A crisis that confirms what foreign audiences already suspected lands with devastating force. A crisis that contradicts the established perception is typically absorbed as an aberration. What determines which of these happens is not the crisis response itself but the *reputational reserves* built in the years before the crisis occurred. A country that has spent a decade building a credible reputation for competent governance absorbs a scandal differently than one whose reputation is already fragile.

This is the quiet thesis that unites everything in this chapter. Public

---

22. In developing a crisis response strategy, SCCT builds on William L. Benoit's image restoration model by identifying primary crisis response strategies — denial, diminishment, and rebuilding — with rebuilding involving compensation of victims, offering apologies, and taking full responsibility. See Benoit, William L. "Image Repair Discourse and Crisis Communication." *Public Relations Review*, vol. 23, no. 2, 1997, pp. 177–186.

relations methodology, applied to nations, is *necessary but insufficient.* The listen-plan-communicate-measure cycle must be run. The Four Models must be used diagnostically. The Barcelona Principles must discipline measurement. Coombs's framework must inform crisis preparation. But none of these instruments, taken together, amount to the full toolkit required to shape a country's image. They are the professional foundation on top of which something larger must be built: a patient, decades-long project of *narrative construction, stakeholder cultivation, and reputational reserve-building* whose payoff arrives long after the practitioners who began it have left the stage. The chapters that follow turn to the elements of that larger project. What this chapter has established is the floor – the minimum professional standard – beneath which no serious national communication effort can afford to fall.

CHAPTER 6
PUBLIC AND CULTURAL DIPLOMACY

WHEN THE STATE SPEAKS TO THE WORLD

T here is a particular moment, familiar to anyone who has worked inside the diplomatic world, when, while looking at the day's news from the host country, one asks the question that defines public diplomacy as a discipline: what are they saying about us, and what can we do about it? The question sounds simple. It is not. Embedded within it are assumptions about who "they" are, what channels might reach them, whether persuasion is even the right goal, and whether the state – the very entity asking the question – is in any position to answer it credibly.

Public diplomacy and cultural diplomacy are the institutional practices through which states attempt to shape their image abroad. They are older than nation branding by several centuries, more constrained by political realities, and more dependent on credibility than almost any other form of communication. Where nation branding borrows the logic of marketing and speaks in the vocabulary of positioning, public diplomacy operates in the harder terrain of policy, legitimacy, and trust. Where branding consultants promise measurable returns on reputation investment, diplomats have always known that the effects of their work are diffuse, delayed, and often invisible until a crisis reveals whether the groundwork was done or not.

This chapter examines the architecture of how states speak to foreign publics. It draws on two frameworks that have become indispensable for anyone thinking seriously about the field: Nicholas Cull's taxonomy of the five components of public diplomacy, and Jan Melissen's reframing of the practice as the New Public Diplomacy, built around networks and dialogue rather than broadcasting alone. It examines the institutional invention that best embodies the field's attempt to solve its own structural credibility problem – the arm's-length cultural institute, from the British Council to the Goethe-Institut to the Alliance Française and the more recent Confucius Institutes.

6.1 PUBLIC DIPLOMACY: DEFINITION, HISTORY, EVOLUTION

Public diplomacy refers to the efforts of governments to inform and influence foreign publics – a distinct activity from traditional diplomacy, which is conducted between governments through accredited diplomats operating largely out of public view. The term itself was coined in 1965 by Edmund Gullion, dean of the Fletcher School of Law and Diplomacy at Tufts University and a distinguished retired foreign service officer, when he established an Edward R. Murrow Center of Public Diplomacy[1] – explicitly as a euphemism that would allow Western democracies to describe their information activities without using the tainted word "propaganda."[2] That origin story matters, because it reveals a tension baked into the field from the outset: public diplomacy has always been both a genuine attempt at something more legitimate than propaganda and a rhetorical rebranding of activities that sometimes look remarkably similar to it.

---

1. Cull, Nicholas J. "'Public Diplomacy' Before Gullion: The Evolution of a Phrase." *USC Center on Public Diplomacy*, 18 Apr. 2006. Cull notes that the earliest surfacing of the phrase appears in a leader piece in the London *Times* in January 1856, where it was used "merely as a synonym for civility" in a piece criticizing the posturing of President Franklin Pierce – a prehistory that qualifies, without overturning, the 1965 origin story.

2. Cull observes that "this new use of an old term was necessary because the even older term 'propaganda'—which Gullion confessed he preferred—had accumulated so many negative connotations." See also Cull, Nicholas J. *The Cold War and the United States Information Agency: American Propaganda and Public Diplomacy, 1945–1989*. Cambridge UP, 2008. The rhetorical work done by the new term is, in this reading, precisely the point: a relabeling strategy designed to insulate Western practice from the associations of interwar and wartime propaganda regimes.

The most useful internal map of the field was proposed by historian Nicholas Cull, who identified five components[3] that together constitute a complete public diplomacy repertoire. These components are (1) listening, (2) advocacy, (3) cultural diplomacy, (4) exchange, and (5) international broadcasting. *Listening* is the systematic monitoring and analysis of foreign public opinion[4] – the often-neglected foundation of the discipline, because you cannot communicate effectively with audiences you do not understand. *Advocacy* is the direct explanation of a country's policies, values, and positions to foreign publics, typically through embassy communications, spokespeople, op-eds, and targeted outreach. *Cultural diplomacy* involves making a country's cultural achievements and everyday life accessible abroad. *Exchange diplomacy* refers to the two-way flow of people – students, scholars, professionals, artists – across borders. And *international broadcasting* is the state-funded projection of news and values through outlets designed for foreign audiences.

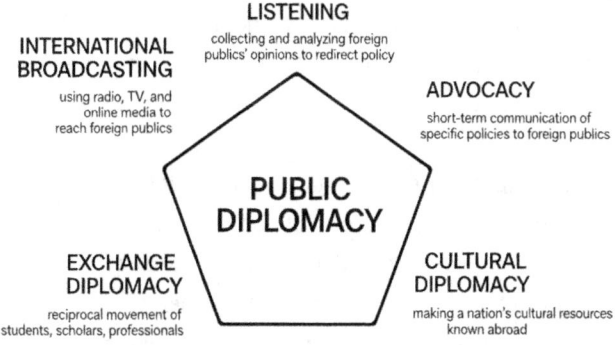

Fig. 9 - Cull's Five Components of Public Diplomacy.

---

3. Cull, Nicholas J. "Public Diplomacy: Taxonomies and Histories." *The ANNALS of the American Academy of Political and Social Science*, vol. 616, no. 1, 2008, pp. 31–54. The article "draws heavily on a report commissioned by the British Foreign and Commonwealth Office in the spring of 2007" and sets out a taxonomy whose five components are "(1) listening, (2) advocacy, (3) cultural diplomacy, (4) exchange, and (5) international broadcasting."
4. Cull treats listening as foundational to effective public diplomacy: it should inform policy choices rather than serve as a mere afterthought, and successful practice requires the systematic integration of feedback mechanisms that connect foreign opinion to policy decisions. See Cull, Nicholas J. *Public Diplomacy: Foundations for Global Engagement in the Digital Age.* Polity, 2019.

The virtue of Cull's framework is its clarity. It separates activities that practitioners and analysts often conflate, and it shows that a serious public diplomacy strategy must operate across all five registers rather than over-specializing in one. Many countries make precisely this mistake: they invest heavily in advocacy and broadcasting – the visible, measurable, press-release-friendly activities – while neglecting listening and exchange, which are the quieter, slower, and ultimately more consequential dimensions of the practice.

Historically, public diplomacy was treated as advocacy plus broadcasting. This is the Cold War model, forged in the ideological competition between the United States and the Soviet Union, institutionalized in bodies like the United States Information Agency and the Voice of America,[5] and mirrored by their Soviet counterparts. The assumption was that the task was essentially one of persuasion: tell your story loudly enough, in enough languages, and the world would come around. The contemporary shift – far from complete – has been toward listening and exchange, reflecting a hard-won recognition that persuasion works much less well than relationship-building, and that a country whose messaging is not anchored in genuine understanding of its audiences will produce noise rather than influence.

The practical question for any state is not which of Cull's five components is most important in the abstract, but where its actual capacity lies and where the gaps are most damaging. A country with world-class cultural institutes but no serious listening apparatus is flying blind. A country with sophisticated monitoring but no exchange programs is watching without touching. A complete strategy balances all five.

---

5. The USIA "was a United States government agency devoted to propaganda which operated from 1953 to 1999," with a primary mission of promoting a favorable view of the United States abroad and focusing exclusively on international audiences until 1990. On Eisenhower's own theory of the agency's credibility problem, see his dictum that "audiences would be more receptive to the American message if they were kept from identifying it as propaganda" – an intuition that avowedly propagandistic materials from the United States might convince few, while the same viewpoints presented through seemingly independent voices would prove more persuasive. See also Cull, Nicholas J. *The Cold War and the United States Information Agency: American Propaganda and Public Diplomacy, 1945–1989.* Cambridge UP, 2008.

6.2 FROM PROPAGANDA TO CONVERSATION

The stated evolution *from propaganda to dialogue* is the core ambition of contemporary public diplomacy theory. No one has articulated it more influentially than Jan Melissen, whose work on what he termed the *New Public Diplomacy*[6] has shaped how ministries, academies, and think tanks talk about the field over the past two decades.

From Old to New Public Diplomacy
(Jan Melissen)

OLD / TRADITIONAL PD	Structural shift from propaganda to networks →	NEW PUBLIC DIPLOMACY
		Multi-actor (states, NGOs, citizens, diasporas)
• State-to-foreign-public		
• One-way information flow		• Two-way dialogic relationships
• Propagandistic logic		• Network logic
• Hierarchical, top-down		• Horizontal, collaborative
• Short-term policy advocacy		• Long-term relationship building

Fig. 10 - Melissen's New Public Diplomacy.

Melissen's reframing is network-based rather than state-centric. In his account, effectiveness in the twenty-first century does not come from broadcasting power alone,[7] or from the vertical projection of official messages from capital to capital. It comes from relationships – with civil society, NGOs, private actors, diaspora communities, cultural institutions, universities, and transnational networks of all kinds. The state, in this

---

6. Melissen, Jan, editor. *The New Public Diplomacy: Soft Power in International Relations*. Palgrave Macmillan, 2005. The volume responds to the post-9/11 global debate on public diplomacy, situating the practice both as a symptom of the rise of soft power in international relations and as a consequence of broader processes of change in diplomatic practice that call for transparency and transnational collaboration.

7. Melissen argues that "the new public diplomacy is here to stay" and that "international actors accept more and more that they have to engage in dialogue with foreign audiences as a condition of success in foreign policy." For a critical extension of this claim, see Hocking, Brian. "Rethinking the 'New' Public Diplomacy." *The New Public Diplomacy: Soft Power in International Relations*, edited by Jan Melissen, Palgrave Macmillan, 2005, pp. 28–43.

view, is no longer the monopolist of its own international image. It is one node in a dense web of actors, some of whom it can coordinate, many of whom it cannot, and all of whom contribute to what foreign publics eventually believe about the country in question.

Applied pragmatically, Melissen's framework has two immediate implications. First, a public diplomacy strategy that ignores its diaspora, its civil society, and its private sector is working with a fraction of its potential bandwidth. Second, the tone of official communication must shift: from *telling* to *asking*, from *broadcasting* to *convening*, from *message discipline* to *relationship management*.

But honesty requires acknowledging that the transformation remains incomplete. Most state communication, even when dressed in dialogic form and participatory language, retains persuasive intent. Consultations are held after decisions are made. Social media accounts use the grammar of conversation while remaining instruments of message discipline. The word "stakeholder" is used to describe audiences who are being informed rather than consulted. Genuine dialogue requires a willingness to be changed by one's interlocutor – and states rarely sustain that willingness on matters of core strategic interest.

This is not a reason to abandon the framework. It is a reason to apply it with realism. The rhetoric of dialogue runs ahead of its practice, but the concept itself has productively shifted expectations about what legitimate public diplomacy should look like. Audiences, especially younger and more digitally sophisticated ones, now notice when a state is broadcasting dressed up as listening. The gap between the rhetoric and the practice is itself a source of credibility damage, and closing that gap – even partially – is one of the clearest opportunities for differentiation available to countries serious about their international standing.

6.3 ACTORS OF PUBLIC DIPLOMACY

Effective public diplomacy is an ecosystem rather than an agency. Four tiers of actors make up the core of that ecosystem, and coordination across them is the operational challenge that defines the field.

The first tier is the foreign ministry itself, which operates the core machinery of public diplomacy through its embassies, information services, press attachés, and, increasingly, dedicated strategic communication units attached to diplomatic missions. This is where the doctrinal center of gravity sits, and where budgets are formally allocated. It is also the tier most constrained by political control and, therefore, most subject to the credibility discount discussed later in this chapter.

The second tier consists of national cultural institutes – bodies like the British Council,[8] the Goethe-Institut,[9] the Institut Français, the Instituto Cervantes, and their various counterparts. These are arm's-length but state-funded, operating in the productive space between government and culture.

The third tier is international broadcasting: the BBC World Service, Deutsche Welle, France 24, NHK World, RT, CGTN, Al Jazeera English, TRT World, and others. These organizations have complex and often controversial relationships with their host states, and they occupy different positions along a spectrum of editorial autonomy. Some, like the BBC World Service, have developed institutional firewalls that afford them a degree of editorial independence widely recognized by international audiences. Others operate with closer alignment to their sponsoring government's messaging priorities. The position of each broadcaster on this spectrum significantly affects the credibility it commands with foreign audiences – and audiences are often more discerning on this point than

---

8. The British Council was established on 5 December 1934 as the British Committee for Relations with Other Countries, renamed the British Council in 1936, and was granted a Royal Charter in 1940. See "Our History." *British Council*. On the Council's arm's-length role, see Taylor, Philip M. "Cultural Diplomacy and the British Council: 1934–1939." *Review of International Studies*, vol. 4, no. 3, 1978, pp. 244–65, where Taylor argues that the Council represented a new and alternative approach to the traditional conduct of foreign affairs based on the practice of cultural diplomacy, predicated on the idea that cultural propaganda would not only enhance British influence and prestige abroad but also further the wider ideals of international understanding.

9. On the post-war architecture of autonomy, see "The Goethe-Institut – In Profile": "When the rebuilding of the Goethe-Institut begins in 1951, the founders at least reflect on the circumstances that made the Akademie so vulnerable to political and ideological appropriation. They therefore choose to set the Goethe-Institut up as a registered association." The structure was intended to protect the institute from being instrumentalized by the state, and the Federal Republic correspondingly chose to organize foreign cultural policy in a decentralized way through non-state intermediary organizations.

state sponsors assume. The spectrum matters enormously, because audiences distinguish between broadcasters in ways that state sponsors sometimes fail to appreciate: a broadcaster that is perceived as independent earns trust that a broadcaster perceived as a mouthpiece can never buy back.

The fourth tier is multilateral and normative: the United Nations system, UNESCO, the OECD, the World Bank's reputational frameworks, and the various indices and rankings that shape how countries are perceived comparatively. A country's standing in the Human Development Index, its UNESCO World Heritage listings, its OECD education scores, its rank in global governance indicators – these are instruments of reputation that no single foreign ministry controls but that every sophisticated public diplomacy strategy must engage with.

The relative weight of these four tiers varies by country and era. Small states often rely heavily on the multilateral tier because it amplifies their voice disproportionately. States with more centralized communication structures tend to invest heavily in broadcasting because it is the tier most amenable to direct coordination. Mid-sized democracies with cultural confidence lean on their cultural institutes. But no country of any international significance operates well on a single tier, and the failures in public diplomacy are most often failures of coordination across tiers rather than failures within any one of them.

6.4 THE CULTURAL INSTITUTE MODEL

The national cultural institute is one of the most distinctive institutional inventions in the history of international relations. The British Council, the Goethe-Institut, the Institut Français and the older Alliance Française,[10]

---

10. The organization was created in Paris on 21 July 1883 under the name *Alliance française pour la propagation de la langue nationale dans les colonies et à l'étranger*. For the colonial and diplomatic genealogy, see Chaubet, François. *L'Alliance française ou la diplomatie de la langue (1883–1914)*. L'Harmattan, 2006. The network's early governing figures – "Ferdinand de Lesseps, Louis Pasteur, Ernest Renan, Jules Verne, Armand Colin… are among the members of the board of directors of the Alliance Française de Paris" – illustrate the blend of scientific, literary, and diplomatic prestige that underwrote the language-as-soft-power model.

the Instituto Cervantes, the Società Dante Alighieri, the Japan Foundation, and more recently the Confucius Institutes[11] – all embody the same basic solution to a structural problem. The problem is that states cannot communicate credibly about themselves, especially on matters of culture and values. The solution is to delegate cultural communication to institutions that are state-affiliated but programmatically autonomous.[12]

The model works best when institutes maintain genuine cultural programming independent of immediate political messaging pressure. The arm's-length structure buys a form of credibility that direct state communication can rarely match. When the Goethe-Institut hosts a reading by a German writer critical of the German government, the credibility dividend flows back to Germany itself – precisely because the institute's autonomy is demonstrated rather than merely claimed. When any cultural institute cancels or censors a program under political pressure from its sponsoring government, the credibility dividend goes sharply into reverse, damaging not only the institute in question but the broader cultural presence of the country it represents. The experience of several Confucius Institutes, where perceptions of restricted academic autonomy led to closures at host universities in multiple countries, illustrates this dynamic with particular clarity.

Different countries have developed distinct variants reflecting different underlying theories of what culture does in the world.

---

11. The first Confucius Institute opened in November 2004 in Seoul, South Korea, after a pilot institute had been established in Tashkent, Uzbekistan in June 2004; the second was opened on the campus of the University of Maryland, College Park. The program has been the subject of sustained international debate regarding the relationship between institutional autonomy and state sponsorship. For a scholarly analysis, see Hartig, Falk. *Chinese Public Diplomacy: The Rise of the Confucius Institute*. Routledge, 2016. On the pace of closures in the United States, see U.S. Government Accountability Office. *China: With Nearly All U.S. Confucius Institutes Closed, Some Schools Sought Alternative Chinese Language Support.* GAO-24-105981, 30 Oct. 2023, gao.gov/products/gao-24-105981, which found that the number of Confucius Institutes at U.S. universities and colleges declined from about 100 to fewer than five between 2019 and 2023.

12. Cull summarizes this insight as one of seven lessons of public diplomacy history: "sometimes the most credible voice in public diplomacy is not one's own." See Cull, Nicholas J. "Public Diplomacy: Seven Lessons for Its Future from Its Past." *Place Branding and Public Diplomacy*, vol. 6, no. 1, 2010, pp. 11–17.

The Cultural Institute Model – The Institutional Answer to the State's Credibility Problem

Institute	Country	Founded	Core Mission
Confucius Institute	China	2004	Chinese language + culture, partnered with universities
Instituto Cervantes	Spain	1991	Spanish language + Hispanic culture
Goethe-Instiut	Germany	1951	German language + contemporary culture
British Council	United Kingdom	1934	English language + cultural relations
Alliance Française	France	1883	French language + Francophone culture

Fig. 11 - The Cultural Institute Model.

The French model is rooted in *cultural universalism* – the idea that French culture carries values (of language, reason, *laïcité*, a certain idea of civilization) that are valuable for the world, not merely for France. The Alliance Française is the older, federated, language-rooted arm; the Institut Français is the newer, more centrally directed complement. The German model, reshaped after 1945, is oriented around *post-war rehabilitation* and the re-establishment of Germany as a cultural and democratic actor – the Goethe-Institut's relatively strong autonomy is not accidental but a deliberate response to the memory of what state-controlled cultural outreach had produced in the 1930s. The British model blends *commercial and cultural functions* in ways that reflect the British Council's history of teaching English for a fee while running cultural programs for soft-power ends. At its peak, the Confucius Institute network operated in more than 150 countries and met a genuine global demand for Chinese language education, particularly in regions where few alternatives existed. However, the model's structural embedding within host universities raised questions about academic autonomy that ultimately proved decisive in several host countries.

The variations reveal the model's range, and the political controversies that attend different choices about autonomy and state proximity. The institute is ultimately a case study in how states *can* communicate credibly: by delegating communication to institutions with a cultural rather than a political identity, and accepting that the price of that credibility is a real degree of autonomy. *Institutes that serve their states best are often those that appear, in any given moment, least obviously to be serving them.*

6.5 CULTURAL DIPLOMACY: THE LONG GAME

Cultural diplomacy is the quietest and, over time, often the most consequential register of public diplomacy. It operates through exchanges, exhibitions, touring performances, film festivals, co-productions, scholarships, language programs, residencies, and long-term educational initiatives. It is the world of Fulbright scholarships,[13] Chevening fellowships, DAAD grants, Erasmus partnerships,[14] and the countless smaller programs that move artists, researchers, and students across borders.

Its effects are diffuse and long-term. Cultural diplomacy builds familiarity where there was none, reduces the suspicion that novelty always provokes, and cultivates future elites who carry positive associations with a country into positions of influence over the following decades. A minister in Nairobi who studied in Berlin, a filmmaker in Buenos Aires who spent a year at a French residency, a journalist in Jakarta whose formative international exposure came through a British Council program

---

13. The Fulbright Program "is one of several United States cultural exchange programs with the goal of improving intercultural relations, cultural diplomacy, and intercultural competence between the people of the United States and other countries through the mutual exchange of persons, knowledge, and skills," and was founded by United States Senator J. William Fulbright in 1946. For an authoritative history, see Johnson, Walter, and Francis J. Colligan. *The Fulbright Program: A History.* U of Chicago P, 1965. On the program's institutional architecture, the binational commission model is widely regarded as the hallmark distinguishing the Fulbright Program from other public or private academic exchange programs (Bureau of Educational and Cultural Affairs, U.S. Department of State).
14. "The 'Erasmus' programme was originally established by the European Union in 1987. It looked to promote closer cooperation between universities and higher education institutions across Europe. This meant setting up an organised and integrated system of cross-border student interchange." See European Commission. "Erasmus to Erasmus+: History, Funding and Future.". On its soft-power function, see the analysis in Feyen, Benjamin, and Ewa Krzaklewska, editors. *The ERASMUS Phenomenon – Symbol of a New European Generation?* Peter Lang, 2013, which examines the program's role in fostering European identity and legitimacy.

– none of these individuals will feel obligated to agree with the foreign policy of the country that hosted them, but all of them carry a texture of association that pure advocacy could never produce.

The mechanism here is relational rather than persuasive. Cultural exposure creates bonds that often survive political tensions between governments, and in some cases even open diplomatic crises. Franco-German cultural programming continued through moments of political disagreement[15] in ways that helped preserve the underlying trust between the two societies. British cultural relations with countries that have sharp disagreements with British foreign policy have been sustained, at the societal level, by institutions whose programming did not disappear when ambassadors were recalled.

Cultural diplomacy is particularly effective because it *partially decouples* from immediate political messaging. A jazz concert, a scholarship, a co-produced documentary – these do not require the audience to agree with the sponsor on anything in particular. The audience's defenses are down, not because they have been tricked, but because there is genuinely nothing to defend against. This reduction in audience resistance is what makes cultural diplomacy reach places that advocacy cannot.

The structural trade-off is that cultural diplomacy produces results that are difficult to measure and easy to cut during budget crises. A decade-long investment in language learning in a distant country will show its value when a generation of local leaders who speak that language is shaping policy – but no quarterly report will capture this, and no annual budget review will find it hard to trim. This makes cultural diplomacy structurally vulnerable. Countries that have sustained it over generations – France and Britain, in particular – have done so by building institutional

---

15. For a treatment of the institutional scaffolding that made such resilience possible, see the Élysée Treaty of 22 January 1963 and the subsequent creation of the Franco-German Youth Office (*Office franco-allemand pour la Jeunesse / Deutsch-Französisches Jugendwerk*), founded on 5 July 1963. See also Defrance, Corine, and Ulrich Pfeil. *Le Traité de l'Élysée et les relations franco-allemandes, 1945–1963–2003*. CNRS Éditions, 2005. Cull treats the Franco-German case as one of his key paired examples in examining successful and unsuccessful uses of each component of public diplomacy ("Public Diplomacy: Taxonomies and Histories," 2008).

arrangements that make cutting difficult, which is precisely the function of the cultural institute model.

6.6 THE CREDIBILITY PROBLEM

All state communication carries an inherent *credibility discount*.[16] Audiences assume self-interest on the part of governments and apply skepticism accordingly, regardless of the specific content of what is being said. This is not cynicism on the part of audiences – it is reasonable *epistemic hygiene*. Governments have interests. Their communications reflect those interests. Any sensible audience factors this into its reception.

The credibility discount varies by country, topic, and audience. Some states are trusted on some topics and systematically distrusted on others: Nordic countries often receive the benefit of the doubt on human rights messaging; major powers with contested foreign policies often do not. Some topics – public health during a non-politicized moment, technical standards, cultural heritage – carry smaller discounts than others. And audiences differ: elite audiences often apply heavier discounts than general publics, while younger digital-native audiences tend to be particularly alert to persuasive framing.

Three strategic principles follow from this structural fact. First, source transparency helps more than source concealment. Audiences accept persuasion from a source they know is persuading them more readily than they accept persuasion disguised as neutral information or organic content. Concealed state communication, when revealed – and it is almost always eventually revealed – produces credibility damage disproportionate to whatever short-term gain the concealment was meant to achieve.

---

16. This insight aligns with Joseph Nye's foundational treatment of soft power. See Nye, Joseph S., Jr. *Soft Power: The Means to Success in World Politics*. PublicAffairs, 2004; and Nye, Joseph S., Jr. "Public Diplomacy and Soft Power." *The ANNALS of the American Academy of Political and Social Science*, vol. 616, no. 1, 2008, pp. 94–109. Cull articulates the institutional corollary that the different elements of public diplomacy locate their sources of credibility in radically different places, and that each ideally requires the appearance of a wholly different relationship to government in order to flourish – structural differences that become critical when a state attempts to administer all its public diplomacy under a single bureaucracy.

Second, third-party voices carry messages that the state itself cannot deliver credibly to foreign publics. Diaspora communities, independent scholars, cultural figures, tourists returning home with stories, independent media telling a country's story from the inside – all of these can communicate things about a country that the country's own government literally cannot say about itself without triggering the credibility discount. Sophisticated public diplomacy understands this and works to enable these voices rather than to control them.

Third, and most importantly, the structural insight of the entire field is that *effective state communication is often communication that visibly is not by the state*. This is the paradox that shapes the architecture of modern public diplomacy: cultural institutes at arm's length, broadcasters with editorial firewalls, exchange programs administered through independent bodies, grants to civil society, support for cultural figures who remain free to criticize. The state that wants to be heard must accept that its most effective voice is one it does not fully own.

This is an uncomfortable conclusion for officials trained in message discipline, and for political leaderships that prefer control to credibility. But it is the central lesson of a century of public diplomacy practice. The state that speaks to the world most successfully is the state that has learned when to speak, when to fund others to speak, and when to step back entirely and let a country's culture, citizens, and institutions speak on its behalf.

That lesson sits at the heart of the distinction between public diplomacy done well and public diplomacy done poorly – and it sets the stage for the chapters that follow, where we turn from the institutional machinery of state communication to the terrain on which all of this work is ultimately tested: the perception of foreign publics, and the broader global competition for attention, trust, and influence.

CHAPTER 7
TELLING A COUNTRY
NARRATIVE, STORYTELLING, AND NATIONAL IDENTITY

I n the early 2000s, South Korea's official promotional campaigns – carefully produced, technically competent, and expensive – were struggling to reach global audiences. Meanwhile, a generation of Korean filmmakers, television producers, and musicians,[1] operating largely outside the orbit of state communication, was beginning to produce work that would, within fifteen years, make Korea one of the most culturally legible countries on earth. By the time *Parasite* won the Academy Award for Best Picture at the 92nd Academy Awards, becoming the first non-English-language film to do so, and won an additional three Oscars, for Best Director, Best Original Screenplay, and Best International Feature Film,[2] and *Squid Game* became Netflix's most-watched series, attracting

1. The Korean Wave, or *hallyu*, refers to the rise in global interest in South Korean popular culture since the 1990s, spread through K-pop, K-dramas, K-beauty, and films, and is widely recognized as a form of soft power and a significant economic asset for South Korea. For a comprehensive overview, see "Korean Wave.". See Kim, Youna. *The Soft Power of the Korean Wave: Parasite, BTS and Drama*. Routledge, 2021.
2. Directed by Bong Joon-ho, *Parasite* won four Oscars at the 92nd Academy Awards – Best Picture, Best Director, Best Original Screenplay, and Best International Feature Film – becoming the first non-English-language film to win Best Picture and the first South Korean film to receive any Academy Award recognition. See Associated Press. "'Parasite' Becomes First Non-English Language Film to Win Best Picture Oscar." *PBS NewsHour*, 9 Feb. 2020.

more than 142 million member households and 1.65 billion viewing hours in its first four weeks[3] the following year, it was obvious that Korea's global image had been radically improved – not by the ministries, but by the storytellers.

This is not a quirk of the Korean case. It is the pattern. Nations are known abroad through the stories[4] that circulate about them, and those stories are almost never the ones that official communicators intended to tell. Cinema, literature, sport, music, games, memes, and the ordinary conversations of diaspora communities do more to shape a country's image than any advocacy campaign – and they do it by a mechanism that official communication, by its nature, struggles to reproduce.

This chapter examines how national narratives function, why some succeed while others fail, and what it means for a country to craft coherent storytelling across radically diverse audiences. Two theoretical instruments anchor the argument. The first is the *narrative transportation theory* of Melanie Green and Timothy Brock,[5] which explains why stories move audiences in ways that arguments cannot. The second is the *Strategic Narrative framework* of Alister Miskimmon, Ben O'Loughlin, and Laura Roselle,[6] which distinguishes the three levels at which national stories

---

3. *Squid Game* pulled in 1.65 billion hours of viewing in 28 days following its September 17, 2021, premiere – 2.6 times the viewership of Netflix's next biggest show, *Bridgerton* Season 1, which generated 625 million hours over its first 28 days. Spangler, Todd. "'Squid Game' Is Decisively Netflix No. 1 Show of All Time With 1.65 Billion Hours Streamed in First Four Weeks, Company Says." *Variety*, 16 Nov. 2021.

4. For the foundational theoretical account of how nations are discursively constructed through shared narrative and print culture, see Anderson, Benedict. *Imagined Communities: Reflections on the Origin and Spread of Nationalism.* Revised ed., Verso, 2006. Anderson defines the nation as "an imagined political community – and imagined as both inherently limited and sovereign," imagined because members will never know most of their fellow-members, yet carry in their minds an image of communion.

5. Green, Melanie C., and Timothy C. Brock. "The Role of Transportation in the Persuasiveness of Public Narratives." *Journal of Personality and Social Psychology*, vol. 79, no. 5, 2000, pp. 701–721. Green and Brock proposed transportation as a mechanism whereby narratives can affect beliefs, defining it as absorption into a story that entails imagery, affect, and attentional focus, and developed a validated transportation scale.

6. Miskimmon, Alister, Ben O'Loughlin, and Laura Roselle. *Strategic Narratives: Communication Power and the New World Order.* Routledge, 2013. The book develops a systematic framework to understand how political actors seek to shape order through narrative projection in the new media environment, exploring how actors form and project narratives and

operate and explains why coherence across those levels is the structural condition for narrative success. Together, they explain why cinema so often does more for a country's image than any campaign,[7] and what the architecture of a coherent national story actually looks like.

7.1 WHY NATIONS TELL STORIES

National storytelling is not a communication supplement. It is a core political function that serves several purposes at once: internal cohesion, external differentiation, political legitimation, and cultural continuity across generations. A nation without a coherent story about itself struggles to mobilize its own citizens, fails to attract outsiders, and loses the ability to interpret its own history to itself during moments of crisis or change.

Stories are the infrastructure through which events, policies, and identities acquire meaning. A policy defended in purely technical terms rarely moves anyone; the same policy framed as the continuation of a national trajectory – as part of *who we are and where we are going* – can mobilize support across divides that no argument could bridge. A political leader who lacks a narrative about the country is reduced to managing events; a leader with one shapes them. This is true inside the country and doubly true outside it, where foreign audiences have even less patience for technical explanations and even greater reliance on the interpretive shortcuts that stories provide.

The storytelling function predates modern communication by millennia. Every nation has accumulated founding myths, heroic narratives, canonical turning points, and collective traumas that are rehearsed in schoolbooks, monuments, public holidays, and the rhythm of political speech. These materials are not raw data awaiting communication; they

---

how third parties interpret and interact with them. See also Miskimmon, Alister, Ben O'Loughlin, and Laura Roselle, editors. *Forging the World: Strategic Narratives and International Relations*. University of Michigan Press, 2017.

7. For the concept of soft power as foreign influence exercised through cultural attraction rather than coercion, see Nye, Joseph S., Jr. *Soft Power: The Means to Success in World Politics*. PublicAffairs, 2004. Soft power lies in the ability to attract and persuade; whereas hard power grows out of a country's military or economic might, soft power arises from the attractiveness of a country's culture, political ideals, and policies.

are already narrative, already interpreted, already doing the work of explaining the country to itself and to outsiders. The communicator arriving in this terrain does not find a blank page. They find an *accumulated manuscript* – partly contradictory, partly outdated, partly still alive – and their task is less one of authorship than of stewardship.

This reframing matters. A country's communicator who understands themselves as the *author* of a national story will tend to produce brittle, top-down messaging that fails to root in the cultural material it depends on. A communicator who understands themselves as a *steward* of a story already being told will listen before speaking, amplify before inventing, and take seriously the fact that the most powerful contributors to national narrative – filmmakers, novelists, athletes, musicians, ordinary citizens with smartphones – are almost never under institutional control.

7.2 NARRATIVE TRANSPORTATION: WHY STORIES CHANGE MINDS

The theoretical mechanism that explains why stories are so powerful was articulated by Melanie Green and Timothy Brock in a series of studies beginning in 2000. Their theory of *narrative transportation* holds that when audiences become immersed in a story, their capacity for counter-argument is reduced and positive emotions can dominate evaluation,[8] and the attitudes produced by that immersion tend to be *more durable* than attitudes produced by explicit persuasion.

Transportation works through cognitive and emotional involvement and the experience of vivid mental images,[9] and a reduced critical stance

---

8. Narrative transportation research shows that transportation produces belief and attitude shifts aligned with story content, reduces counterarguing against story claims, and leads to long-term effects on attitudes after the story ends.

9. When people are transported to narrative worlds and captivated, they may experience strong emotions, vivid mental images, and a loss of awareness of their surroundings or the passage of time – the "lost in a story" phenomenon at the core of narrative transportation theory, which defines transportation as a combination of attention, imagery, and feelings. Green, Melanie C. "Transportation into Narrative Worlds." *Entertainment-Education Behind the Scenes: Case Studies for Theory and Practice*, edited by Lauren B. Frank and Paul Falzone, Palgrave Macmillan, 2021, pp. 87–101.

during narrative consumption. While you are reading a novel or watching a film, your cognitive defenses are not raised against the worldview implicit in what you are consuming; you are *inside* the experience rather than evaluating it from the outside. Attitudes, assumptions, and associations acquired during transportation slip past the filters that would block them if they arrived as a direct claim.

NARRATIVE TRANSPORTATION THEORY
(Green & Brock, 2000)

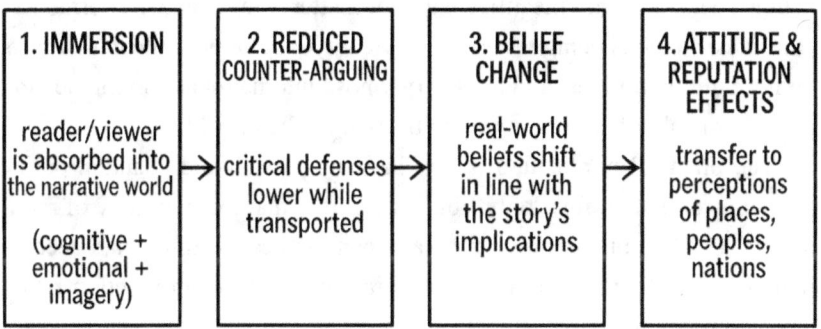

1. IMMERSION	2. REDUCED COUNTER-ARGUING	3. BELIEF CHANGE	4. ATTITUDE & REPUTATION EFFECTS
reader/viewer is absorbed into the narrative world (cognitive + emotional + imagery)	critical defenses lower while transported	real-world beliefs shift in line with the story's implications	transfer to perceptions of places, peoples, nations

Fig. 12 - *Narrative Transportation (Green & Brock).*

Applied pragmatically to the question that animates this book – how countries build international influence – the implications of transportation theory are substantial and slightly uncomfortable for institutional communicators.

First, national narratives that transport audiences shift perceptions more durably than factual or argumentative communication does. A viewer who has spent ten hours inside a Danish crime drama has acquired a set of associations about Denmark – about its landscapes, its institutions, its social texture, its moral imagination – that no embassy briefing and no tourism advertisement could install with comparable depth. Those associations will condition how the viewer interprets Danish news stories for years.

Second, this explains why cultural export consistently outperforms institutional messaging in reputational terms, even when the scale of deliberate investment is far smaller. A modestly funded national cinema industry that produces two or three internationally successful films in a decade will do more for its country's image than a much larger public diplomacy budget spent on campaigns. The ratio is not a small multiple; it is often an order of magnitude.

Third, and most difficult for policy communicators to accept, this means that *emotional and narrative content outperforms rational argumentation* at shaping durable perception. The ministry official trained to emphasize facts, statistics, and policy substance is working against the grain of how human attitude formation actually operates in relation to nations. This does not mean facts do not matter – they matter enormously when a narrative is being tested against reality – but it does mean that facts do not build narratives, and a country whose international communication consists mainly of reciting its strengths will not be heard.[10]

The practical implication is not that countries should abandon policy communication and fund only filmmakers. It is that the hierarchy of reputational impact puts narrative first, and communicators must plan accordingly – supporting, enabling, and aligning with cultural production rather than competing with it through official channels.

7.3 THE NARRATIVE CORE: FINDING THE DEEP STORY

Every enduring national narrative has a *core*: a fundamental story about who the nation is, where it came from, and what it stands for at the level of identity. Think of the core not as a slogan but as a *premise* – the deepest assumption from which everything else follows.

The most developed contemporary framework for analyzing how national narratives actually work is the *Strategic Narrative theory* of Alister Miskimmon, Ben O'Loughlin, and Laura Roselle. Their contribution is to distinguish three levels at which national stories operate.

---

10. Green and Brock observed that public narrative predominates over public advocacy in everyday experience: novels, films, soap operas, music lyrics, and stories in newspapers and television command far more waking attention than advertisements, sermons, editorials, and billboards, and the persuasive impact of narratives on real-world beliefs has long been recognized. Green and Brock, "The Role of Transportation," pp. 701–703.

- *System narratives* tell a story about how the international order is organized:[11] is the world a community of cooperating states, a theater of civilizational competition, a liberal order under threat, a multipolar equilibrium emerging from a redistribution of global influence? Every country communicates, implicitly or explicitly, a story about what kind of world it sees itself in.

- *Identity narratives* tell a story about *who the nation is*: a reluctant great power, a cultural civilization, a commercial republic, a revolutionary vanguard, a small country that punches above its weight, a post-colonial state reclaiming its voice. These stories are the deepest layer and the hardest to change.

- *Issue narratives* tell stories about specific questions: why this war, why this trade policy, why this climate position, why this alliance. Issue narratives are the visible surface of strategic communication, but they draw their force from the levels beneath them.

Strategic Narratives – Miskimmon, O'Loughlin & Roselle

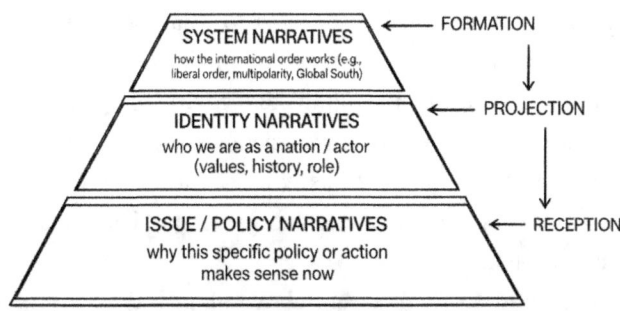

Fig. 13 - Strategic Narrative (Miskimmon, O'Loughlin, Roselle).

---

11. For the tripartite distinction among system, identity, and issue narratives, see Roselle, Laura, Alister Miskimmon, and Ben O'Loughlin. "Strategic Narrative: A New Means to Understand Soft Power." *Media, War & Conflict*, vol. 7, no. 1, 2014, pp. 70–84. The authors argue that soft power in its widely understood form has become a straitjacket, overly focused on assets rather than on how influence takes place, and that strategic narrative gives intellectual purchase on the complexities of international politics, especially regarding how influence works in a new media environment.

The value of the Miskimmon–O'Loughlin–Roselle framework is that it explains why national narratives succeed or fail. They work when the three levels cohere. They fail when identity narratives contradict system narratives, or when issue narratives contradict identity narratives. A country that tells an identity story of openness while taking issue positions of closure will be heard as incoherent. A country that describes the international system as cooperative while conducting itself in ways that contradict that vision will forfeit credibility on both levels. *Coherence across the three levels is not a stylistic virtue; it is a condition of being believed.*

The narrative core lives at the identity level but connects upward to the system narrative and downward to issue narratives. It is rarely explicit. It lives as the common premise beneath specific campaigns, films, political speeches, and cultural products. Japan's narrative core – something like "an old culture reconciled with modernity, attentive to craft, reticent but confident" – is never stated in a sentence, yet it is recognizable across film, design, cuisine, diplomacy, and advertising. Ireland's core blends literary tradition, diasporic warmth, and a particular relationship to language and place. These cores are not *invented* by committees. They are *discovered*.

Discovering the core requires listening to what the country says about itself when it is *not* trying to persuade – in its art, sport, humor, and internal conflicts. What do its filmmakers return to when they are not thinking about export? What do its comedians mock, and what do they treat as sacred? What do its novelists write about obsessively? The narrative core is visible in these places more clearly than in any strategic communications plan.

Attempts to impose a core from above almost always fail. The core emerges organically and is only named, refined, and amplified by deliberate communication. The communicator's job is not to invent it but to recognize it, protect it from being flattened into slogans, and align institutional messaging with what is already being said by the country's own cultural life.

7.4 VECTORS OF NATIONAL NARRATIVE

National narrative travels through specific channels, each with its own temporal rhythm and reach.

Cinema and streaming drama have become the primary vectors of national narrative[12] in the contemporary attention economy – more influential than any official communication channel that any government operates.[13] A single globally successful series can install a set of national associations in hundreds of millions of minds with a depth that no advocacy campaign could match. The Korean wave, the Nordic noir phenomenon,[14] the earlier waves of Italian neorealism and French *nouvelle vague*, the persistent global presence of Indian cinema, the remarkable global reach of Turkish serials across the Middle East, the Balkans, and Latin America[15] – each of these has shaped how the coun-

---

12. For a specific examination of streaming drama's role in projecting national image, see Jin, Dal Yong. "Korea's Cultural Diplomacy and the Political Economy of Soft Power." *Asian Perspective*, vol. 46, no. 1, 2022, pp. 93–117. See also the observation that since the 2000s, the Korean Wave has transformed from a phenomenon driven primarily by satellite broadcasts to one driven by social media and the internet, with foreign-language subtitles of K-dramas and real-time translations of K-pop performances broadening the scope of Korean pop culture.

13. On how nation branding often fails when it substitutes messaging for substance, see Anholt, Simon. "Beyond the Nation Brand: The Role of Image and Identity in International Relations." *Exchange: The Journal of Public Diplomacy*, vol. 2, no. 1, 2013, pp. 6–12. Anholt argues that there are no shortcuts: only a consistent, coordinated, and unbroken stream of useful, noticeable, world-class, and above all relevant ideas, products, and policies can, gradually, enhance the reputation of the country that produces them.

14. Outside the Nordic region, the twenty-first-century crime boom coincided with a wider fascination with the Nordic welfare states and "all things Nordic," and the publishing and media industries benefited greatly from the global Nordic "brand" – making Nordic crime fiction both an intermedial genre and a twenty-first-century global brand. Stougaard-Nielsen, Jakob. "Nordic Crime Fiction." *Nordics.info*, Aarhus University, 2025. See also Gulddal, Jesper, and Stewart King. "On Top of the World: Mapping the Nordic Crime Fiction Boom Based on Translation Data." *Translation Studies*, 2024.

15. Turkish dramas have seen significant growth since the 2000s, and Turkey surpassed Mexico and Brazil as the second-largest exporter of television series after the United States by the mid-2010s, with the industry playing a crucial role in increasing Turkey's popularity in Asia, Europe, Latin America, and North Africa. See Parrot Analytics. "The Global Influence of Television: From *The White Lotus* to Turkish Dramas." *Parrot Analytics*, 18 Feb. 2025.

tries in question are perceived with a durability that official communicators cannot rival.

Literature operates more slowly but more deeply. Novels, poetry, and serious nonfiction shape intellectual elites – journalists, academics, policymakers, editors – whose perceptions cascade into wider publics over generations rather than years. The literary reputation of a country is a *slow-burning asset* that compounds over decades; countries that have invested in translation programs, literary festivals, and international recognition for their authors tend to enjoy reputational benefits long after the specific investments are forgotten – as demonstrated by the global success of Nordic crime fiction.[16]

Sport offers episodic but powerful narrative moments. Olympics, World Cups, international championships, and, increasingly, globally followed league competitions concentrate attention on national identity for brief but intense periods. The images produced in these moments – athletes, stadiums, crowds, winners – are absorbed by global audiences with a vividness that is hard to produce by any other means. But sport is also volatile: a successful performance lifts the national image temporarily, while a hooliganism scandal or a corruption revelation damages it just as sharply.

Mega-events – World Expos, European Capital of Culture designations, state visits, international summits, anniversaries of historical turning points – provide orchestrated platforms for narrative projection.[17] Their advantage is concentration and control; their disadvantage is limited dura-

---

16. Nordic Noir – crime fiction from the Nordic region – is one of the most significant international publishing stories of the twenty-first century, often associated with Stieg Larsson's *Millennium* trilogy (with global sales exceeding 100 million) and forming part of a wave of hundreds of books by Nordic crime writers that have experienced success beyond their countries of origin. Gulddal, Jesper, and Stewart King. "On Top of the World: Mapping the Nordic Crime Fiction Boom Based on Translation Data." *Translation Studies*, Taylor & Francis, 2024.

17. On sport and major events as concentrated platforms for soft-power projection, *hallyu* has served as South Korea's third diplomatic pillar since 2010, exemplified by the 2018 Pyeongchang Olympics, which showcased Korean culture and attracted global attention. Joh, Sung-wook. "Hallyu as Soft Power: The Success Story of the Korean Wave and Its Use in South Korea's Foreign Policy." Academia.edu, 2021. See also Nye, Joseph S., Jr. "Soft Power." *Foreign Policy*, no. 80, 1990, pp. 153–171.

tion and high cost. They are *inflection points* rather than *infrastructure*, and countries that rely on them alone tend to experience reputation as a series of spikes rather than a sustained presence.

No single vector operates in isolation, and the strongest reputational effects come from cross-reinforcement across multiple channels. When a country's cinema, literature, sport, and cultural exports all point in recognizably the same direction, each vector strengthens the credibility of the others. When they contradict each other, the reputation they produce is fragmented and weaker than the sum of its parts.

7.5 NARRATIVE COHERENCE ACROSS AUDIENCES

A national narrative must resonate simultaneously with radically different audiences: citizens and foreigners, elites and mass publics, friends and adversaries, close neighbors and distant observers. The challenge is not small. A story that works in Berlin may not work in Jakarta; a story that moves domestic citizens may be illegible or alienating abroad; a story that pleases diplomatic elites may fail completely with mass publics who distrust elites in general.

Maintaining coherence while translating across contexts requires identifying which elements of the narrative carry across cultures and which require substantial reframing. *Universal human experiences* – family, loss, ambition, humor, the weight of history on the present – translate widely. Specific political vocabularies, historical references, and internal controversies often do not. A narrative that leans on material in the second category will feel *parochial* abroad, while a narrative that abandons specificity in pursuit of universality will lose the distinctiveness that made it worth telling in the first place.

There are two failure modes. *Over-translation* produces narratives smoothed to fit foreign frames so thoroughly that they lose what made the country distinctive in the first place – a country presented as just another pleasant destination, with no edges, no texture, no memory. *Under-translation* produces narratives that resonate only domestically and feel hermetic or self-absorbed abroad – a country talking to itself in public. Both fail, and both are common.

The functional test of narrative coherence is whether a foreigner who has engaged with the country's cultural output across multiple touchpoints – a film, a novel, a sporting event, a visit – would perceive a consistent national identity. The test is not whether each touchpoint says the *same thing*, but whether together they produce a *recognizable sensibility*.

Coherence, in other words, is not uniformity. It is *family resemblance across varied expressions*, held together by the narrative core and recognizable through shared sensibility rather than identical content. A country's cinema and its cuisine do not need to say the same thing; they need to feel like they come from the same place.

7.6 THE UNCONTROLLABLE POLYPHONY

No institution controls the totality of what is said about a nation. Citizens, diasporas, tourists, journalists, adversaries, and the country's own internal dissenters all contribute narratives that extend beyond any official reach. Digital media has amplified this polyphony dramatically, giving individual voices global reach and enabling counter-narratives to scale rapidly against institutional messaging. A single viral video, a single well-crafted investigative piece, a single thread of diaspora memoirs can shape global perception in ways that no ministry can match and no embassy can counter.

This is, for many state communicators, the hardest feature of the contemporary environment to accept. The instinct when facing polyphony is to seek control – to push harder on official channels, to respond rapidly to every counter-narrative, to attempt to dominate discourse about the country. This instinct is almost always counterproductive. The attempt to dominate produces precisely the impression of *manipulation* that the country was trying to avoid, while consuming resources that would have been better spent on the kinds of deep narrative investment that actually shape perception over time.

The sensible institutional response is not to suppress polyphony – an impossible task – but to ensure that the official narrative is strong enough, and the country's cultural production vigorous enough, that the whole ecosystem holds together without needing to suppress dissent. Internal dissent is itself part of the national narrative.[18] Countries that visibly tolerate criticism of themselves, that allow their own writers to savage their failings, that produce journalism that holds power accountable, generally emerge with stronger international reputations than countries that prioritize message uniformity over public debate. *The attempt to suppress critical voices tends to produce reputational damage greater than the criticism itself would have caused if allowed to circulate.* This is not a moral observation; it is an empirical regularity across decades of comparative national reputation data.

The mature view of national narrative accepts polyphony as a structural feature of contemporary reputation and works *with* it rather than *against* it. It understands that the official voice is one voice among many, that its comparative advantage lies in consistency and credibility rather than volume, and that the most powerful things ever said about a country are almost always said by people the country does not employ.

This concession to reality is not a defeat. It is the beginning of a more realistic and, ultimately, more effective practice – one that sets the conditions under which good stories can be told by many different voices, and trusts that the cumulative effect, over time, will carry further than any single campaign could.

---

18. Analysis of the Nation Brands Index data suggests that the main driver of a positive national image is the perception that a country contributes to the world beyond its own borders – that it is a principled, collaborative actor; this effect cannot be achieved by messaging, but must be consistently and substantially proved by real behavior over the long term. As Anholt sums up: "if you want to be admired, be admirable". Anholt, Simon. Interview by Nicholas J. Cull. "Anholt and Cull, Part Three: Good News for Sweden, Canada, and the World." *USC Center on Public Diplomacy*, 15 Dec. 2020.

CHAPTER 8
THE DIGITAL
AND PLATFORMS
DIGITAL CONVERSATIONS
BETWEEN NATIONS IN
THE PLATFORM ECONOMY

T here was a time, not long ago in historical terms, when a country could reasonably believe it controlled its own story. Ministries of foreign affairs drafted *communiqués*, cultural institutes programmed exhibitions, tourism boards commissioned campaigns, and state broadcasters beamed curated images across borders.[1] Between the nation and the world stood a manageable roster of gatekeepers – correspondents, editors, broadcasters, diplomats – through whom the official narrative passed, sometimes faithfully, sometimes critically, but always within a recognizable architecture of mediation. That architecture has collapsed.

What has replaced it is not a new system of control but the permanent absence of one. National reputation in the digital era is not broadcast; it is conversation.[2] It is not transmitted; it is negotiated, contested, remixed,

---

1. The classical architecture described here corresponds to what Joseph Nye terms state-centered «public diplomacy», historically structured around unidirectional broadcasting to foreign publics. Nye emphasizes that effective public diplomacy requires listening as well as talking and that soft power rests on shared values – a framing that already anticipates the collapse this chapter describes. See Nye, Joseph S., Jr. "Public Diplomacy and Soft Power." *The Annals of the American Academy of Political and Social Science*, vol. 616, no. 1, 2008, pp. 94–109.
2. This reconceptualization parallels Manuel Castells's theory of «mass self-communica-

and occasionally hijacked. A teenager with a smartphone in Seoul, a disgruntled tourist in Lisbon, a political dissident in exile in a Western city, and a food blogger in Mexico City are all, whether they know it or not, producing fragments of their countries' international images at scales that rival – and frequently surpass – the output of entire ministerial apparatuses. The central task of this chapter is to map this landscape, identify its operational logic, and extract the practical consequences for anyone charged with shaping a country's global standing.

8.1 THE DISSOLUTION OF INSTITUTIONAL CONTROL

The old regime of national communication rested on a simple premise: scarcity. Producing content capable of crossing borders required resources – printing presses, transmission licenses, correspondents, budgets – that only institutions possessed. Scarcity concentrated authorial power in a small number of hands, and this concentration is what made institutional communication strategy coherent. One could plan a campaign because one could plausibly identify the channels through which a message would travel.

That premise is gone. Platforms have dissolved the scarcity of global distribution. Any user, anywhere, with a free account and a modest device, possesses technical capacity once reserved for news agencies. The gatekeepers have not disappeared – legacy media still shape agendas, especially in times of crisis – but they have been joined, outflanked, and frequently overruled by a chaotic plurality of non-institutional voices.

The most useful conceptual response to this dissolution is Gini Dietrich's PESO model,[3] which has become the standard framework for thinking about communication once the old binary of paid and earned

---

tion», a new communication system that, he argues, has emerged with the rise of interactive, horizontal networks built on the Internet and wireless platforms, and through which insurgent politics and social movements can intervene more decisively in the new communication space. See Castells, Manuel. *Communication Power*. Oxford UP, 2009.

3. Dietrich introduced the term PESO – paid, earned, shared, and owned media – in her 2014 book *Spin Sucks*, which advocates for honest and open communications within public relations. See Dietrich, Gini. *Spin Sucks: Communication and Reputation Management in the Digital Age*. Que Publishing, 2014.

media ceased to describe reality. PESO organizes the field into four integrated categories: *paid media* (advertising and sponsored content), *earned
media* (third-party editorial coverage), *shared media* (content on platforms
and user-generated material that circulates socially), and *owned media*
(channels directly controlled by the communicator, such as official
websites, newsletters, or institutional social accounts).[4]

PESO Model – Gini Dietrich

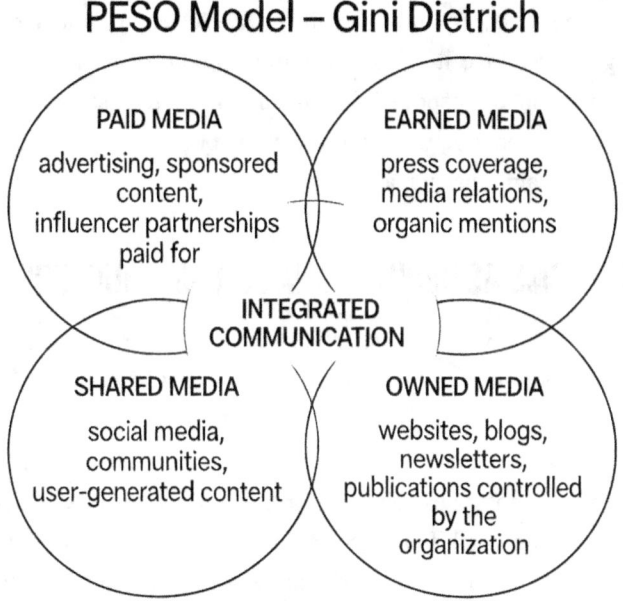

Fig. 14 - PESO Model (Dietrich).

The analytical power of PESO for national reputation lies in its
acknowledgment that shared and owned media now carry reputational
weight that once belonged almost exclusively to earned coverage. Even a
brief piece of user-generated video about a country's everyday life can
shape perceptions more profoundly than a thoughtful feature in a respected
broadsheet. An Instagram Reel by a diaspora creator can reach audiences
that no ministerial press office will ever address. The center of gravity in

---

4. For an authoritative overview of the model's evolution, see Dietrich's own framing of
PESO as an integrated approach to paid, earned, shared, and owned media that has been
continually updated since its launch a decade ago. Dietrich, Gini. "What Is the PESO
Model©?" *Spin Sucks.*

communication strategy has shifted, and strategies built on the old earned-paid dichotomy are not merely incomplete – they are structurally misaligned with the environment in which they must operate. The practical implication for nation-branding practitioners is a reorientation of the institutional role. Ministries and official communicators have not become irrelevant; their relevance has changed shape.

Their value lies less in producing content than in curating, amplifying, contextualizing, and responding within a PESO environment rather than attempting to sit above it. This is a diminishment of power in one sense and an expansion of responsibility in another: the institution that once authored the national narrative must now become its most intelligent reader and most agile participant.

8.2 PLATFORMS AS REPUTATIONAL INFRASTRUCTURE

There remains a temptation, especially among senior officials formed in earlier media cultures, to treat platforms as neutral conduits – updated versions of the postal service through which content flows unaltered. This assumption is wrong in ways that have serious operational consequences.

Platforms are not pipes. Their algorithms actively shape which images of a country gain visibility and which remain effectively invisible. A photograph of a beach in Vietnam that performs well on the engagement metrics embedded in Instagram's ranking system will reach millions;[5] an equivalent photograph that does not trigger those metrics will reach almost no one. The algorithm is not a passive transmitter but an active editor, and it edits according to logics that have nothing to do with the public interest of any nation.

Those logics are well understood in their broad outlines. Algorithmic systems privilege engagement – reactions, shares, comments, dwell time –

---

5. Tarleton Gillespie's foundational work situates platforms as active curators rather than neutral conduits: "Algorithms ... play an increasingly important role in selecting what information is considered most relevant to us, a crucial feature of our participation in public life." See Gillespie, Tarleton. "The Relevance of Algorithms." *Media Technologies: Essays on Communication, Materiality, and Society*, edited by Tarleton Gillespie et al., MIT Press, 2014, pp. 167–94.

because engagement is the currency that platforms sell to advertisers. This preference systematically favors content that is emotionally provocative, visually striking, controversial, or unusually distinctive. It disfavors the patient, the complex, the nuanced, and the institutionally mediated. A country whose genuine story is one of gradual social progress, technical competence, or quiet cultural richness will find itself algorithmically disadvantaged relative to countries whose imagery is more spectacular, more conflictual, or simply more photogenic.

This creates what we might call the distortion pressure of platform infrastructure. The attention economy rewards novelty and distinctiveness, pushing national imagery toward the stereotypical, the extreme, or the visually sensational.[6] Countries that learn to produce content that satisfies algorithmic preferences achieve visibility; those that do not become, for vast global audiences, effectively invisible – not because their stories are absent from the world, but because the infrastructure through which those stories must travel does not surface them.

Commercial imperatives layer additional distortions. A country that invests in well-crafted Instagram advertising becomes visible through one set of aesthetic conventions; a country whose image circulates primarily through news coverage becomes visible through another. The platform is not reporting reality; it is constructing a particular slice of visibility governed by its business model.

The operational consequence is straightforward: national reputation is now co-produced with algorithmic systems.[7] Any serious strategy must therefore begin with a diagnostic of how a given country currently

---

6. The concept underlying the phrase "attention economy" was first articulated by Herbert A. Simon, who observed that "in an information-rich world, the wealth of information means a dearth of something else: a scarcity of whatever it is that information consumes," namely "the attention of its recipients." See Simon, Herbert A. "Designing Organizations for an Information-Rich World." *Computers, Communications, and the Public Interest*, edited by Martin Greenberger, Johns Hopkins UP, 1971, pp. 37–72.

7. This argument extends Gillespie's claim that algorithms should be understood not merely as code with consequences but as a socially constructed and institutionally managed mechanism for assuring public knowledge – a new knowledge logic that competes with, and may be supplanting, the editorial logic that has long governed public information. See Gillespie, "The Relevance of Algorithms," cited above.

performs across platform logics, not merely an inventory of what the country would like the world to know about itself. The two are different projects, and confusing them is among the most common and most expensive errors in contemporary nation-branding practice.

8.3 THE DIGITAL DIASPORA

Diasporic communities have always influenced the image of their countries of origin.[8] Remittance economies, returning migrants, cultural associations, and exile communities have shaped perceptions across centuries. What digital platforms have done is to transform diaspora communication from an intermittent, locally anchored phenomenon into a continuous, globally distributed nation-branding operation conducted largely without central direction.

The contemporary diaspora is not merely present online; it produces content at volume, in multiple languages, across every available platform. This content takes many forms: personal narratives of adaptation and identity, cultural celebration during national holidays, political critique of home-country leadership, humor directed at national stereotypes, culinary demonstrations, musical performances, and commentary on current events. All of it reaches, simultaneously, two distinct audiences: host-country audiences who encounter the homeland through a diasporic lens, and compatriots still living in the home country, who see their own nation reflected back through expatriate eyes.

The reputational weight of this content is substantial, and the reason is perceptual. A single TikTok sequence about a country's street food scene can shape perceptions more profoundly than a thoughtful feature in a respected broadsheet.[9] Audiences read diaspora content as authentic lived

---

8. On the digital transformation of diasporic nation-branding, see the observation that digital platforms have strengthened the ties binding diasporic communities and now allow large numbers of diasporas to interact, share experiences, and develop a sense of community and belonging. See Bjola, Corneliu, Ilan Manor, and Geraldine Asiwome Adiku. "Diaspora Diplomacy in the Digital Age." *Routledge International Handbook of Diaspora Diplomacy*, edited by Liam Kennedy, Routledge, 2022, pp. 334–46.
9. Empirical work confirms that "individuals tend to value more authentic messages over polished marketing messages" and respond more positively to user-generated content from

experience – as testimony rather than messaging.[10] This perceived authenticity grants it a credibility that institutional communication structurally cannot achieve. A ministry's tourism campaign announces; a diaspora creator witnesses. The difference matters.

The complication for national communication strategy is that diaspora narratives frequently diverge from official ones. An emigrant community may celebrate aspects of home-country culture that the current government does not prioritize, critique policies that the government defends, or articulate national identity in terms that contradict official framing. The result is the coexistence of multiple, competing images of the same country, some of which may overshadow the state-produced version.

Pragmatically, this requires a shift in how governments relate to their diasporas – from treating them as constituencies to be informed, or as sources of remittances, to engaging them as reputational actors whose content shapes how the country is seen. This does not mean attempting to control diaspora expression, which is usually impossible and almost always counterproductive. It means building relationships, providing cultural resources, recognizing creative work, and accepting that the national narrative will be polyphonic rather than unitary. Countries that engage their diasporas intelligently gain credible amplifiers; countries that ignore or antagonize them acquire articulate critics with international audiences.

---

peers and micro-influencers than to traditional advertising. See Younis, Dina. "How User-Generated Content Shapes Brand Authenticity and Consumer Trust." *Athens Journal of Mass Media and Communications*, vol. 11, 2025, pp. 1–11.

10. The perceptual privilege granted to authenticity is well-established in source-credibility research; see, e.g., the finding that "authenticity is critical for influencers because it affects the extent to which users trust them and eventually determines user engagement with their generated content," and that sponsorship can undermine perceived authenticity by signaling extrinsic motivation. See Audrezet, Alice, Gwarlann de Kerviler, and Julie Guidry Moulard. "Authenticity under Threat: When Social Media Influencers Need to Go beyond Self-Presentation." *Journal of Business Research*, vol. 117, 2020, pp. 557–69.

8.4 CITIZEN BRANDING: THE NATION TOLD BY ITS INHABITANTS

If the diaspora speaks of the nation from abroad, the citizenry speaks of it from within, and at equally formidable scale. Tourists photograph, students vlog, workers document, creators build audiences, and the aggregate result is a continuous stream of content that constitutes a substantial portion of any country's contemporary international image.

The reputational weight of citizen-produced content rests on the same perceptual logic as diaspora content: it registers as unmediated experience rather than orchestrated messaging. A traveler's complaint about bureaucratic harassment at an airport will circulate and be believed; a ministry's denial will not displace it. A creator's loving documentation of regional cuisine will do more for tourism than any brochure. The content is credible precisely because it is visibly uncoordinated.

Some of this content is produced by individuals who have, over time, become *de facto* nation branders. Food creators, travel vloggers, cultural commentators, political analysts, and lifestyle influencers build audiences around national themes, and in doing so shape international perceptions on a scale that official bodies cannot match. They operate without mandate, without accountability, and without coordination with any state apparatus. Their loyalty is to their audiences, their craft, and their commercial interests – not to any reputation strategy. Yet their cumulative impact is often decisive.

The implication, which practitioners often resist because it complicates their professional self-understanding, is that a country's international image depends substantially on the lived experiences and expressive capacities of its own citizens. A country whose citizens have good lives, meaningful work, creative tools, and positive relationships with visitors will tend to produce content that reflects those conditions. A country whose citizens are frustrated, restricted in expression, or marginalized will produce content that reflects those conditions too.

This suggests a conclusion that may be uncomfortable for communication professionals but that follows directly from the evidence: policies that improve citizens' lives and provide them with expressive tools may do more for national reputation than most dedicated reputation campaigns. Investment in education, cultural infrastructure, quality of public services, and digital literacy is not unrelated to national image – it is, increasingly, its primary determinant. Communication strategy operates on a foundation that communication strategy alone cannot build.

8.5 SOCIAL LISTENING AND SENTIMENT ANALYSIS

One of the genuine advances of the digital era is analytical. Platforms generate, as a by-product of their operation, a continuous and global signal about how a country is perceived – searchable, archivable, and analyzable at scales unimaginable two decades ago. The infrastructure of social listening now available to reputation practitioners includes tools that aggregate mentions across languages, classify sentiment, identify emerging narrative clusters, track the propagation of specific framings, and flag early indicators of reputational shift.[11]

Used well, this infrastructure permits a degree of situational awareness that would have seemed fantastical to the communication officers of an earlier era. A country can, in principle, know within hours that a new negative narrative is forming in a specific market,[12] identify the communities driving it, assess its likelihood of reaching mainstream coverage, and prepare responses calibrated to the actual state of public perception rather than to institutional assumptions about it.

The operative word, however, is *in principle*. In practice, the widespread adoption of listening tools has produced a characteristic pathology: measurement as substitute for judgment. Dashboards proliferate, reports

---

11. On the current industry landscape of such tools, see the observation that "social media sentiment analysis reveals how people feel about your brand, not just how often they talk about it," with AI-based tools now analyzing tone, language, and context across platforms at scale. McLachlan, Stacey. "12 Social Media Sentiment Analysis Tools for 2026." *Hootsuite Blog*, 20 Jan. 2026.

12. The *in principle* caveat is well-supported by industry reporting. See the claim that social media listening tools "track every relevant brand mention, even if you are not tagged," allowing organizations to identify and address conversations that could harm reputation while amplifying those that generate positive sentiment. Sprout Social. "Best Social Media Listening Tools for Your Brand in 2026.".

accumulate, sentiment scores fluctuate, and practitioners mistake the resulting visibility of data for strategic clarity. The fact that a country's sentiment score has dropped by six points in a given market does not, by itself, tell anyone what to do. It requires interpretation – of why, of whether the shift matters, of what action if any would improve the situation, and of what action would make it worse.

Effective listening combines quantitative signal with qualitative interpretation. It treats data as an input to reasoning rather than a replacement for it. It asks not only what the numbers say but what they mean, and it recognizes that meaning is always contextual, always contested, and never self-evident. The practitioners who extract value from listening infrastructure are those who hold the data lightly, read it with cultural literacy, and resist the institutional temptation to confuse a well-designed dashboard with a well-understood situation.

8.6 REPUTATIONAL CRISIS IN THE VIRAL ERA

All of the preceding dynamics compress and accelerate under conditions of crisis. Viral propagation has reduced the timeline of reputational damage from weeks to hours and expanded its reach from regional to global within a single news cycle.[13] A video filmed by a tourist, a comment by a minor official, a leaked document, a contested image – any of these can, under the right conditions, seize global attention and lodge itself in collective memory before any institutional response is even possible.

Classical crisis playbooks, developed in an era when audiences formed judgments over days rather than minutes, fail against these dynamics. By the time an official statement is drafted, cleared, translated, and released, the narrative has already stabilized in the minds of global audiences, and

---

13. Empirical industry data support this compression: "social media backlash can strike any brand without warning, turning a minor misstep into a full-blown crisis within hours," with research indicating that 96% of brand crises spread internationally within 24 hours. See "Effective Crisis Management Strategies for Social Media for PR and Brand Pros." *5W PR Agency Blog*, 23 Oct. 2025.

revising it requires disproportionate effort. Facts, in the viral era, arrive late to their own story.

Effective crisis management under these conditions depends less on response capacity than on pre-built narrative infrastructure:[14] credible spokespeople already known to international audiences, standing relationships with foreign journalists that permit rapid context-setting, authorization protocols that allow decisions in minutes rather than days, and pre-tested framings for recurrent categories of incident. Countries that construct this infrastructure in calm periods can act in crisis periods; countries that have not, cannot, regardless of the talent of their communicators.

The deeper truth, however, is that crisis response is usually not where national reputation is won or lost. Prevention matters more than response, and what prevents a crisis from causing lasting damage is not the quality of the reaction but the reputational reserves accumulated over years. A country that has built a deep, credible, multi-sourced positive image across diaspora, citizen, institutional, and earned channels can absorb a viral crisis the way a strong currency absorbs a speculative attack.[15] A country whose reputation is shallow, single-sourced, or already contested will find even a minor incident metastasizing into lasting harm.

This is perhaps the central strategic lesson of the chapter. Digital platforms have made national reputation faster, more volatile, and more uncontrollable than at any point in modern history. The response is not to attempt to reimpose a control that is no longer available, but to build the conditions – authentic citizen experience, engaged diaspora, competent institutional presence, analytical literacy, narrative infrastructure – from

---

14. Case studies in reputation management confirm the premium on speed plus prior preparation. See the example of American Airlines, which activated its social crisis protocol within an hour of a critical January 2025 incident – posting updates, deploying support resources, and sharing a video message from its CEO – a response widely cited as an example of crisis communication done well. Sprinklr. "6 Social Media Crisis Management Strategies for 2025." *Sprinklr*, 3 July 2025.

15. The Anholt Nation Brands Index data illustrate that even highly ranked nations can experience sharp reputational shifts in relatively short periods – with single-year drops of seven, eleven, or as many as thirty-one positions recorded following major geopolitical events or domestic political shifts. See Kinsman, Jeremy. "The World Loves More Canada: Simon Anholt's New Nation Brands Index." *Policy Magazine*, 31 Oct.

which a credible international image can continuously regenerate itself, regardless of which story happens to go viral next.

The country that understands this has already begun to adapt. The country that does not will spend the next decade explaining itself to audiences that have already made up their minds.

CHAPTER 9
ARTIFICIAL INTELLIGENCE

THE FUTURE OF
NATIONAL REPUTATION?

Every previous chapter of this book has assumed a particular kind of informational world – one in which national images, however contested, were produced by human beings[1], circulated through human-mediated channels, and interpreted by human audiences. That assumption no longer holds. Artificial intelligence has inserted itself into every layer of the reputational stack[2]: producing content, mediating encounters, analyzing perceptions, fabricating evidence, and orchestrating campaigns at scales and speeds that no human organization can match.

---

1. This framing echoes Simon Anholt's long-standing argument that national reputation is a product of lived national identity rather than marketing. Anholt coined the term "nation brand" in 1996 to indicate that a country's reputation behaves rather like the brand images of companies and products, but later introduced the concept of "Competitive Identity" in response to the misinterpretation that a country's image could be reduced to marketing techniques. See Anholt, Simon. *Competitive Identity: The New Brand Management for Nations, Cities and Regions*. Palgrave Macmillan, 2007.

2. For an overview of how AI mediation has reshaped information encounters, see Gillespie, Tarleton. "The Relevance of Algorithms." *Media Technologies: Essays on Communication, Materiality, and Society*, edited by Tarleton Gillespie, Pablo J. Boczkowski, and Kirsten A. Foot, MIT Press, 2014, pp. 167–94; and Narayanan, Arvind. "Understanding Social Media Recommendation Algorithms." Knight First Amendment Institute, Columbia University, 9 Mar. 2023.

The consequence is not an incremental change in how reputation works but a transformation of the environment in which reputation forms at all.

This closing chapter examines that transformation. It takes the pragmatic view that AI is neither a neutral tool to be deployed nor an existential threat to be feared, but an infrastructural reality that must be understood and navigated. It introduces the analytical framework – *Coordinated Inauthentic Behavior* – that has emerged as the dominant operational response to the new environment. And it closes on the question this book has been circling from its opening pages: in a world where national images are generated by systems no one fully controls, what does it still mean for a country to have a reputation, and who can credibly claim to be responsible for it?

9.1 AI AS ENVIRONMENTAL TRANSFORMATION, NOT TOOL

The first analytical error to avoid is the framing of AI as a tool. Tools are acquired, deployed, and set aside; they sit in the hands of their users and serve intentions external to themselves. AI does some of these things, but reducing it to a tool misses the more important fact: AI has become part of the *environment* in which informational encounters occur. It does not sit in the communicator's hand so much as in the medium through which every message now travels.

Consider how a typical user in London, São Paulo, or Jakarta now forms a first impression of an unfamiliar country. They type a query into a search engine that ranks results through machine-learned relevance models[3]. They read summaries generated by large language models before they reach primary sources. They consume automatically translated text whose choices have shaped nuance and connotation. They watch videos recommended by algorithmic systems optimizing for engagement. They

---

3. Narayanan's influential essay on recommender systems provides context on this shift. In computer science, the algorithms driving social media are called *recommender systems*, and these algorithms are the engine that makes Facebook and YouTube what they are, with TikTok more recently showing the power of an almost purely algorithm-driven platform. See Narayanan, Arvind. "Understanding Social Media Recommendation Algorithms." *Knight First Amendment Institute*, Columbia University, 9 Mar. 2023.

may converse with a chatbot that synthesizes information across thousands of sources into a single confident paragraph. Each of these interactions is mediated by machine intelligence, and each shapes the impression that forms.

This mediation is not neutral. AI systems encode the patterns present in their training data, including accumulated biases about nations – which countries are described as dynamic or stagnant, safe or dangerous, modern or traditional, reliable or corrupt[4]. These framings, inherited from decades of published text, crystallize into *statistical associations*[5] that the model reproduces whenever a country is mentioned. The output feels objective because it arrives without a visible author, but it is no more neutral than the corpus from which it was learned.

The operational reframing required is therefore not «how do we use AI in our communication strategy?» but «how do we exist as a country within an AI-mediated informational world?». The first question assumes agency we no longer exclusively possess. The second acknowledges that national reputation is now co-produced with machine intelligences no government fully controls or audits, and it orients strategy toward the more difficult but more realistic task of navigating that co-production.

---

4. This claim is empirically supported by computational studies. Nationality bias has been identified as a source of significant bias in peer evaluations, and easy-to-obtain examples of obvious bias from language models include associations linking specific nationalities to stereotypical traits — such as assumed political values or presumed linguistic abilities — biases rooted in the culture of the writers or speakers whose thoughts are expressed in the training corpus. See Navigli, Roberto, et al. "Biases in Large Language Models: Origins, Inventory, and Discussion." *ACM Journal of Data and Information Quality*, vol. 15, no. 2, June 2023, article 10, pp. 1–21.

5. A large-scale empirical study found structural cultural bias in major LLMs. A disaggregated evaluation of cultural bias for five widely used large language models (OpenAI's GPT-4o, GPT-4-turbo, GPT-4, GPT-3.5-turbo, and GPT-3) found that all models exhibit cultural values disproportionately resembling those of English-speaking and Protestant European countries — a finding that reflects the composition of training corpora rather than any inherent cultural hierarchy, though cultural prompting as a control strategy can improve the cultural alignment of the models' output for 71–81% of countries and territories. See Tao, Yan, et al. "Cultural Bias and Cultural Alignment of Large Language Models." *PNAS Nexus*, vol. 3, no. 9, September 2024.

9.2 HOW LANGUAGE MODELS CRYSTALLIZE NATIONAL IMAGES

Large language models warrant particular attention because they are becoming a primary interface through which global audiences encounter information about countries. Understanding how they produce the images they produce is essential to any serious reputation strategy.

The mechanism is, at a technical level, straightforward. Language models are trained on enormous corpora of text drawn from the web, books, news archives, academic publications, and other sources. These corpora contain countless existing representations of every country – travel accounts, political analysis, fiction, journalism, social media posts, Wikipedia articles, tourism materials. The training process compresses this varied material into statistical patterns of association, which the model reproduces when queried about a specific nation.

The consequence is systematically uneven. Countries that enjoy rich, varied, high-quality representation in the textual record – those with extensive academic literature, diverse journalistic coverage, abundant cultural production translated into major languages, and prominent presence across digital archives – appear in model outputs as complex, multifaceted entities. Their histories are rendered with nuance, their societies with internal differentiation, their contemporary lives with dynamic specificity. Countries with thinner representation appear *flat*[6]. Their descriptions collapse into a handful of dominant associations, often stereotypical, sometimes outdated, frequently filtered through a narrow band of external observers rather than domestic voices.

This is a reputational issue of considerable strategic weight. Representation in training data has become a form of soft power[7], directly shaping

---

6. This reflects a systemic issue documented in recent scholarship on AI equity. Despite advances, AI models continue to be geared toward the needs of English-speaking people in high-income countries, with one of the main training-data sources for generative AI — the Common Crawl archive of around 300 billion web pages — strongly skewed toward English content. See Zorthian, Julia. "Large Language Models Are Biased – Local Initiatives Are Fighting for Change." *Nature*, 28 Nov. 2025.

7. This extends Joseph Nye's classical framework into the algorithmic domain. Soft power is the ability to influence or persuade others through the use of attractive means rather than

how a country appears in the AI-mediated information environment that an increasing share of the world's population now inhabits. A country can run elegant tourism campaigns across every platform and still, when a user in Berlin asks a chatbot «what is life like in [that country]?», receive a summary that reflects 1990s travel writing[8] and decades-old political commentary. The campaign reaches audiences who seek it out; the chatbot reaches audiences who are merely curious, and there are orders of magnitude more of the latter than the former.

Practical responses exist, though none offer complete solutions. Governments and cultural institutions can invest in expanding the quantity and quality of domestically produced content in widely spoken languages and in formats accessible to crawlers that populate training corpora. They can support academic and journalistic production that reflects contemporary national realities. They can engage directly with AI developers regarding representation concerns, a channel that is beginning to open but remains underdeveloped. These efforts will not reshape model outputs overnight, but they can, over time, shift the *textual substrate* from which future models learn.

9.3 AI AS ANALYTICAL TOOL

If AI transforms the environment, it also offers genuine analytical capability to those navigating that environment. At this register – AI as instrument rather than atmosphere – the opportunities are substantial and largely real.

Analytical systems can now process millions of articles, social media

---

force or coercion – a process entailing the strategic shaping of others' preferences through culture, political values, and foreign policies; Nye himself observed that in the Information Age, credibility is the scarcest resource. See Nye, Joseph S., Jr. *Soft Power: The Means to Success in World Politics*. PublicAffairs, 2004.

8. On why this outdated representation persists, see the expanded treatment in Gallegos, Isabel O., et al. "Bias and Fairness in Large Language Models: A Survey." *Computational Linguistics*, vol. 50, no. 3, September 2024, pp. 1097–1179. The data used to train an LLM may be drawn from a non-representative sample of the population, which can cause the model to fail to generalize well to some social groups, and the data may omit important contexts where proxies used as labels may incorrectly measure the actual outcome of interest.

posts, and documents across dozens of languages in near real time. They can identify sentiment patterns, track narrative evolution, cluster topics, detect emerging frames, and map the geographic and demographic distribution of perceptions about a country. They can compare national reputation across markets, flag divergences between how a country perceives itself and how it is perceived abroad, and surface shifts invisible to the human eye precisely because those shifts occur across scales no human could manually survey.

Predictive applications extend further. Models can forecast the likely trajectory of reputational indicators based on current signal, simulate counterfactual scenarios to estimate the impact of proposed communication actions, and test strategies against modeled audience segments before actual deployment. Used competently, these capabilities can raise the quality of strategic decisions meaningfully.

The caveats, however, are serious, and they echo the warning offered in the previous chapter about social listening[9]. Analytical systems excel at detecting what can be *quantified*; they are much weaker at the qualitative, affective, and cultural shifts that often drive reputation in ways that resist metrics. A country's image can decay in ways that show up clearly in sentiment scores only well after the underlying erosion has occurred, and it can improve through slow cultural currents that no topic model will surface until they have already transformed the situation.

The prudent stance treats AI analytics as amplification of human judgment rather than its replacement. The systems provide powerful input to decisions that still require interpretation, cultural literacy, ethical reflection, and the kind of contextual understanding that remains distinctively human. Institutions that invest in analytical infrastructure without simulta-

---

9. For a foundational counterpoint on the limits of metrics-driven analysis, see Kavanagh, Jennifer, and Michael D. Rich. *Truth Decay: An Initial Exploration of the Diminishing Role of Facts and Analysis in American Public Life.* RAND Corporation, 2018. Over the past two decades, public discourse in the United States has been characterized by "Truth Decay," defined as increasing disagreement about facts, a blurring of the line between opinion and fact, an increase in the relative volume of opinion compared with fact, and lowered trust in formerly respected sources of factual information – trends whose damaging consequences include the erosion of civil discourse and political paralysis.

neously investing in the interpretive capacity to use it well tend to produce impressive dashboards and poor decisions.

9.4 DEEPFAKES AND GEOPOLITICAL DISINFORMATION

The most alarming reputational threat introduced by AI is synthetic media – convincing video, audio, and imagery of events that never occurred, produced at costs that have fallen dramatically and continue to fall. What once required significant technical resources can now be generated by any individual with basic skills and consumer-grade hardware[10]. The implications for national reputation are substantial.

The most visible threat is *fabricated evidence* targeting national leadership or institutions: a synthesized video of a head of state appearing to announce a policy never adopted, a manipulated recording of a minister appearing to utter statements never made, a forged document presented as a leak from within a ministry, a falsified video of a protest engineered to suggest unrest that did not occur. Each of these can be produced rapidly, disseminated through existing amplification infrastructure, and consumed by audiences before any verification process can engage.

The structural problem is that detection technology consistently lags production technology[11]. Each advance in synthetic media generation prompts an advance in detection, but detection arrives later, requires technical expertise audiences do not possess, and must compete with emotional responses that often form before debunking circulates. During

---

10. On the scale of this shift, see Colman, Ben. "Detecting Dangerous AI Is Essential in the Deepfake Era." *World Economic Forum*, 9 July 2025. As Colman documents through cases such as the 2024 Arup deepfake fraud, the fundamental challenge lies in the asymmetric arms race between increasingly accessible generation tools and detection capabilities that consistently lag behind, a dynamic that the World Economic Forum's *Global Cybersecurity Outlook 2025* identifies as a critical test of trust in an AI-powered world.

11. This dynamic is well documented in the computer-vision literature. Deep learning techniques have capitalized on the large amounts of real and fake data available online, but since training detection algorithms depends on fake data created by generation tools, deepfake detectors lag behind generators; consequently, the development of detection algorithms provides direct feedback to generation algorithms on what makes deepfakes detectable and can encourage adversarial generation to bypass detection. See Pei, Gan, et al. "The Tug-of-War Between Deepfake Generation and Detection.".

this lag – which is frequently the entire lifespan of a news cycle – false content lodges in memory, shapes perception, and influences judgment in ways that later correction cannot fully reverse.

A second effect, subtler and ultimately more corrosive, is what scholars have come to call the *liar's dividend*[12]: the general awareness of synthetic media enables bad actors to dismiss genuine evidence as fabricated. A real video of official misconduct can be deflected as a deepfake[13]. A genuine document can be denounced as a forgery. The cumulative effect is an erosion of trust in documentation and witness testimony as such, which benefits those who wish to act without accountability and harms those whose legitimacy depends on verifiable record.

Defending national reputation against this environment requires capacities that most governments have not yet built: forensic detection infrastructure[14], rapid-response institutions authorized to issue technical verifications within hours, international coordination networks to share attribution intelligence, and sustained public literacy campaigns that help citizens and foreign audiences reason about media they encounter. These are expensive, institutionally demanding investments, and the political constituency for funding them is thin. It will not remain thin indefinitely.

---

12. The originating legal scholarship is Chesney, Robert, and Danielle Citron. "Deep Fakes: A Looming Challenge for Privacy, Democracy, and National Security." *California Law Review*, vol. 107, no. 6, 2019, pp. 1753–1820. The *liar's dividend* is a concept coined by legal scholars Bobby Chesney and Danielle Citron, who suggest that the existence of actual, and increasingly realistic, deepfakes can make false claims of misinformation more credible. For recent empirical confirmation, see also Schiff, Kaylyn Jackson, Daniel S. Schiff, and Natália S. Bueno. "The Liar's Dividend: Can Politicians Claim Misinformation to Evade Accountability?" *American Political Science Review*, vol. 119, no. 1, 2025, pp. 71–90.

13. The Schiff, Schiff, and Bueno five-study experimental series confirms this empirically. The study addresses the phenomenon of *misinformation about misinformation*, or politicians "crying wolf" over fake news – strategic and false claims that stories are fake news or deepfakes may benefit politicians by helping them maintain support after a scandal; five survey experiments with over 15,000 American adults found that claims of misinformation raise politician support across partisan subgroups. These findings, drawn exclusively from a U.S. sample, may not generalize uniformly across different political cultures.

14. The emerging open technical standard in this space is the C2PA framework. The *Coalition for Content Provenance and Authenticity*, or C2PA, provides an open technical standard for publishers, creators, and consumers to establish the origin and edit history of digital content. See Coalition for Content Provenance and Authenticity. *C2PA Technical Specification*, version 2.3, 2024.

9.5 ALGORITHMIC NARRATIVE WARFARE

The synthesis of AI production, algorithmic amplification, and platform infrastructure has produced an operational domain that did not exist a decade ago: algorithmic narrative warfare. State and non-state actors now conduct campaigns that generate content automatically, amplify it through networks of coordinated accounts[15], target it precisely to receptive audiences, and sustain it across months or years – all at scales and speeds that human communication teams cannot match.

The intellectual and operational challenge these campaigns pose is severe. Attempting to respond by adjudicating truth fails on two counts. First, it is *slow*: by the time a claim has been evaluated, contextualized, and countered, the narrative has already propagated. Second, it is *philosophically awkward*: many of the most effective campaigns combine accurate material with misleading framing, making binary true-or-false judgments inadequate to the actual communication pathology in play.

The framework that has emerged as the dominant operational response is *Coordinated Inauthentic Behavior*, a category first formalized by Meta in 2018[16] and subsequently adopted, with variations, by most major platforms, research institutions, and an expanding set of governments. The CIB framework makes a crucial analytical move: it stops trying to judge content by its truth or viewpoint and starts judging accounts and networks by whether they are being coordinated[17] and whether the identities behind them are concealed.

The reasoning behind this shift is pragmatic. Speech in a democracy

---

15. Several state actors have been identified by government and independent reports as major sources of foreign disinformation, employing tactics that include networks of fake social media accounts and websites with hidden operators and hidden connections to foreign governments, disseminated through state-run propaganda, social media, and artificial intelligence – including deepfakes. See United States, Government Accountability Office. *Foreign Disinformation: Defining and Detecting Threats*. GAO-24–107600, 2024.

16. The originating document is Gleicher, Nathaniel. "Coordinated Inauthentic Behavior Explained." *Meta Newsroom*, 6 Dec. 2018. Coordinated Inauthentic Behavior (CIB), a term coined by Facebook in 2018, is a category of influence operation that has gained widespread attention in recent years. For scholarly critique, see Douek, Evelyn. "What Does 'Coordinated Inauthentic Behavior' Actually Mean?" *Slate*, 2 July 2020.

17. Meta's formal policy articulates this principle directly. Where adversarial threat actors

includes the right to be wrong, to hold unpopular views, and to express them vigorously. Trying to adjudicate truth at scale therefore risks suppressing legitimate expression and invites accusations of censorship. But orchestration and identity concealment are different matters. A network of accounts pretending to be independent citizens of one country while in fact being operated centrally from another country is doing something objectively identifiable regardless of what the accounts are saying. The CIB frame targets *orchestration* rather than *opinion*, which makes it both more operationally tractable and more defensible as a governance principle.

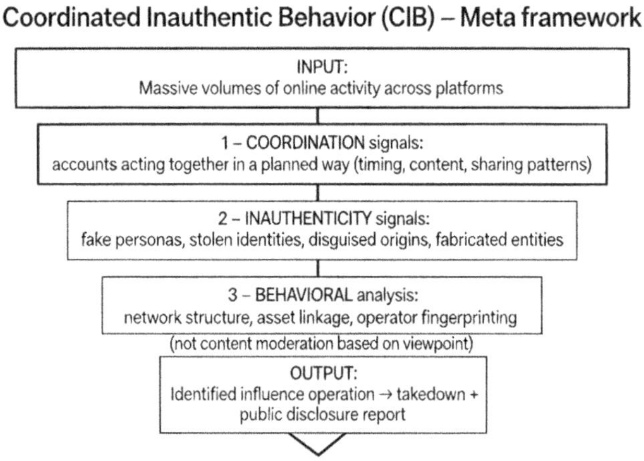

Coordinated Inauthentic Behavior (CIB) – Meta framework

INPUT:
Massive volumes of online activity across platforms

1 – COORDINATION signals:
accounts acting together in a planned way (timing, content, sharing patterns)

2 – INAUTHENTICITY signals:
fake personas, stolen identities, disguised origins, fabricated entities

3 – BEHAVIORAL analysis:
network structure, asset linkage, operator fingerprinting
(not content moderation based on viewpoint)

OUTPUT:
Identified influence operation → takedown +
public disclosure report

Fig. 15 - Coordinated Inauthentic Behavior (CIB) Detection.

Since 2018, CIB detection has become the operational category around which platform enforcement, academic research, and government response increasingly organize themselves. Platforms publish regular CIB takedown reports. Research institutions maintain CIB databases[18] and develop detec-

use false identities to engage in sophisticated forms of inauthentic behavior, they engage in what has been defined as Coordinated Inauthentic Behavior (CIB), with these enforcement actions and standards applied *agnostic of content or ideology*. See Meta Platforms, Inc. "Inauthentic Behavior." *Transparency Center*, 2024.

18. Research institutions have developed increasingly sophisticated typologies. Meta has narrowed its definition of CIB to the extent that most activities once falling under that label are now allowed or at least are not considered "inauthentic"; instead, Meta's focus has shifted to coordinating "adversarial actors," leaving others on-platform, while recent literature

tion methodologies. Governments have begun to fold CIB frameworks into their foreign interference responses.

The framework is not a complete solution. Attribution remains structurally difficult[19]: identifying the true origin of coordinated campaigns requires forensic and intelligence resources that most countries cannot independently deploy, and sophisticated actors layer their operations to obscure provenance. Detection itself lags the pace of new operations, which evolve to evade identified patterns. And CIB frameworks, being descriptive rather than normative, tell us *what* orchestration is occurring without telling us *what to do about it* beyond removing accounts.

Nonetheless, CIB represents the most productive response the field has developed to a threat that moves too fast for truth-adjudication to keep up. For any country building a defensive posture against narrative warfare, engagement with the CIB framework – its methodologies, its research networks, its emerging governance structures – is now table stakes rather than an advanced option.

9.6 DEFENSE, GOVERNANCE, AND THE CLOSING QUESTION

Protecting national reputation in the AI-mediated environment requires institutional capacity that most countries have not yet developed, funded, or politically prioritized. The defensive architecture, at minimum, includes: continuous monitoring of how AI systems represent the country in their outputs; structured intervention to improve representation in training data substrates; forensic capability to detect synthetic media and

---

addresses coordination extending beyond influence operations and including both authentic and inauthentic cases. See Rogers, Richard, and Nicola Righetti. "Coordinated Inauthentic Behaviour on Facebook? A Typology of Manufactured Attention." *Sage Journals*, 2025.

19. On the politics and technical challenges of attribution, see Hedling, Elsa, and Hedvig Ördén. "Disinformation, Deterrence and the Politics of Attribution." *International Affairs*, vol. 101, no. 3, 2025, pp. 967–986. Disinformation, like cyber attacks, stems from the digital age, and both are sometimes referred to as "hybrid threats" or tools of "hybrid warfare," though they differ in methods and objectives; cyber attacks target technological systems directly, whereas disinformation targets human perception and information environments, and like cyber attacks, disinformation operations introduce difficulties with attribution of who, what, and potentially why an attack occurred.

coordinated campaigns targeting the country; rapid-response institutions empowered to verify or refute viral content within the time windows that matter; and standing international partnerships through which intelligence, methodologies, and technical capacity can be shared.

The governance architecture extends further. No country can unilaterally address an environment shaped by globally operating platforms and globally distributed actors. The emerging agenda includes shaping international norms on synthetic media – including provenance standards, labeling requirements, and accountability for malicious use[20] –, establishing meaningful platform accountability for amplification choices, requiring transparency in algorithmic promotion of political content, and building common forensic infrastructure through which smaller countries can access capabilities they could not independently maintain.

This is structurally multilateral work. It requires alliances among countries that may have divergent interests on many issues but share an interest in a minimally trustworthy information environment. It requires engagement with platforms as *quasi-public infrastructure* whose governance choices have geopolitical consequences. It requires the slow, patient negotiation of shared standards across jurisdictions that legislate differently and value different things. None of this is fast. All of it is necessary.

And this returns us to the question this book has been circling from its first page: *in a world where national images are generated by systems no one fully controls, what does it still mean for a country to have a reputation?*

The answer is neither as despairing as the scale of the transformation might suggest nor as optimistic as communication professionals accustomed to managing narratives might hope. A country's reputation, in the AI era, is no longer something it authors. It is something it participates in, contests for, cultivates, defends, and at times must simply endure. The

---

20. The emerging normative landscape is surveyed in United States, National Security Agency. *Content Credentials: Strengthening Multimedia Integrity in the Generative AI Era.* Cybersecurity Information Sheet, January 2025. The C2PA specification is being advanced toward adoption as an ISO international standard, marking a significant milestone in content authenticity and integrity, and the specification is also being examined by the W3C for adoption at the browser level.

forces shaping it include state action, institutional communication, citizen expression, diaspora voice, algorithmic amplification, machine generation, and adversarial orchestration – all operating simultaneously, at different speeds, under different logics.

Within this environment, the country that does well is not the one that *controls* its image – because that project is finished – but the one that maintains the most authentic, varied, credible, and resilient substrate of reality from which its image can continuously regenerate. Real citizens living real lives. Real institutions doing real work competently. Real culture produced and circulated without coercion. Real relationships with diasporas, with neighbors, with international publics. Real analytical honesty about how the country is actually perceived and why.

Reputation in the AI era is, in this sense, less about *storytelling* than about being «the kind of country whose story tells itself well» – and building the institutional capacity to ensure that, when others try to tell a different story, the original remains credible enough to hold.

Responsibility for this project cannot be consolidated in any single actor. Governments matter, but cannot do it alone. Institutions matter, but cannot substitute for citizens. Citizens matter, but require conditions that only collective action can provide. Diasporas matter, but must be engaged, not instrumentalized. Platforms and AI developers matter, but cannot be expected to optimize for the public interest of nations whose residents they do not primarily serve. The responsibility is distributed, and distributed responsibility is the hardest kind to organize – which is precisely why the countries that organize it well will, in the decades ahead, exercise an influence disproportionate to their size, their wealth, or their traditional instruments of power.

ABOUT THE AUTHOR

Carmelo Cutuli is a specialist in external and institutional relations with extensive international experience, having consolidated a deep expertise in the field of internationalization. For over a decade, he led the international communication and marketing activities of the «Italian Consortium of Quality Handicrafts», a regionally-owned company, overseeing the design and management of numerous promotional projects abroad, particularly in the United States.

Among his overseas engagements, he has operated as Senior Advisor for several North American public relations agencies and served on the board of the «Italian-American Chamber of Commerce of the Midwest». Particularly active in the associative landscape, he has held leading positions in Italy for prominent U.S. non-profit organizations, including «Civitan International» and the «Order Sons and Daughters of Italy in America» (OSDIA), where he currently serves as President of the Rome Chapter. He is also President for Southern Italy of «Confassociazioni» and Vice President of «Confassociazioni International», with delegated responsibility for institutional relations with the United States, Canada, and Australia.

Registered with the «Ordine dei Giornalisti del Lazio» (Order of Journalists of the Lazio Region), he complements his institutional activity with a prolific editorial output: he is a regular contributor to both Italian- and English-language publications and the author of several essays devoted to topics in Communication Sciences. His works published in English include: *Successful Italian American Business People: From Immigrant Dreams to Business Titans. The Remarkable Journey of Italian Americans in Entrepreneurship.* TWS, 2023; *The World to Come: Trends and Chal-*

lenges in the New Globalization (with Deiana, A.). Giacovelli International Editions, 2023; *How to Manage Business Relations with Italy: A Reasoned Overview of Italian Institutional Players Supporting International Business*. TWS, 2022; *The Startupper Mindset: Harnessing the Power of Entrepreneurial Thinking*. TWS, 2022; and *The Italian Global Trade System: The Italian Foreign Trade Network Explained to International Entrepreneurs and Investors*. TWS, 2022.

BIBLIOGRAPHY

Anderson, Benedict. *Imagined Communities: Reflections on the Origin and Spread of Nationalism*. Rev. ed., Verso, 2006.

Anholt, Simon. "Beyond the Nation Brand: The Role of Image and Identity in International Relations." *Exchange: The Journal of Public Diplomacy*, vol. 2, no. 1, 2013, pp. 1–7.

Dinnie, Keith. *Competitive Identity: The New Brand Management for Nations, Cities and Regions*. Palgrave Macmillan, 2007.

Armitage, Richard L., and Joseph S. Nye, Jr. *CSIS Commission on Smart Power: A Smarter, More Secure America*. Center for Strategic and International Studies, November 2007.

Aronczyk, Melissa. *Branding the Nation: The Global Business of National Identity*. Oxford UP, 2013.

Bauder, Harald. "Benedict Anderson's Imagined Communities." *Critical Legal Thinking*, 25 Apr. 2023, criticallegalthinking.com/2023/04/25/benedict-andersons-imagined-communities/.

Benoit, William L. "Image Repair Discourse and Crisis Communication." *Public Relations Review*, vol. 23, no. 2, 1997, pp. 177–186.

Berglund, Karl, Jesper Gulddal, and Stewart King. "On Top of the World: Mapping the Nordic Crime Fiction Boom Based on Translation Data." *Translation Studies*, vol. 17, no. 2, 2024, pp. 83–104, doi.org/10.1080/14781700.2024.2333737.

Billig, Michael. *Banal Nationalism*. Sage Publications, 1995.

Cannadine, David. "The Context, Performance and Meaning of Ritual: The British Monarchy and the 'Invention of Tradition', c. 1820–1977." *The Invention of Tradition*, edited by Eric Hobsbawm and Terence Ranger, Cambridge UP, 1983, pp. 101–64.

Castells, Manuel. *Communication Power*. Oxford UP, 2009.

Cevik, Serhan, and Tales Padilha. "Measuring Soft Power: A New Global Index." *IMF Working Paper No. 24/212*, International Monetary Fund, October 2024, doi.org/10.5089/9798400289576.001.

Chesney, Robert, and Danielle Citron. "Deep Fakes: A Looming Challenge for Privacy, Democracy, and National Security." *California Law Review*, vol. 107, no. 6, 2019, pp. 1753–1820.

Cohen, Bernard C. *The Press and Foreign Policy*. Princeton UP, 1963.

Coombs, W. Timothy. "Protecting Organization Reputations During a Crisis: The Development and Application of Situational Crisis Communication Theory." *Corporate Reputation Review*, vol. 10, no. 3, 2007, pp. 163–176.

Coombs, W. Timothy, and Sherry J. Holladay. "Helping Crisis Managers Protect Reputational Assets: Initial Tests of the Situational Crisis Communication Theory." *Management Communication Quarterly*, vol. 16, no. 2, 2002, pp. 165–186.

Cull, Nicholas J. *The Cold War and the United States Information Agency: American Propaganda and Public Diplomacy, 1945–1989*. Cambridge UP, 2008.

Cull, Nicholas J.. *Public Diplomacy: Foundations for Global Engagement in the Digital Age.* Polity Press, 2019.

Cull, Nicholas J.. *Public Diplomacy: Lessons from the Past.* CPD Perspectives on Public Diplomacy, USC Center on Public Diplomacy, 2009.

Cull, Nicholas J.. "Public Diplomacy: Taxonomies and Histories." *The ANNALS of the American Academy of Political and Social Science*, vol. 616, no. 1, 2008, pp. 31–54.

Defrance, Corine, and Ulrich Pfeil. *Le Traité de l'Élysée et les relations franco-allemandes, 1945–1963–2003.* CNRS Éditions, 2005.

Dietrich, Gini. *Spin Sucks: Communication and Reputation Management in the Digital Age.* Que Publishing, 2014.

Dinnie, Keith. *Nation Branding: Concepts, Issues, Practice.* Butterworth-Heinemann, 2008.

Douek, Evelyn. "What Does 'Coordinated Inauthentic Behavior' Actually Mean?" *Slate*, 2 July 2020, slate.com/technology/2020/07/coordinated-inauthentic-behavior-facebook-twitter.html.

Entman, Robert M. "Framing: Toward Clarification of a Fractured Paradigm." *Journal of Communication*, vol. 43, no. 4, 1993, pp. 51–58.

Faloyin, Dipo. *Africa Is Not a Country: Breaking Stereotypes of Modern Africa.* Harvill Secker, 2022.

Fiske, Susan T. "Stereotype Content: Warmth and Competence Endure." *Current Directions in Psychological Science*, vol. 27, no. 2, 2018, pp. 67–73.

Fiske, Susan T., et al. "A Model of (Often Mixed) Stereotype Content: Competence and Warmth Respectively Follow from Perceived Status and Competition." *Journal of Personality and Social Psychology*, vol. 82, no. 6, 2002, pp. 878–902.

Gallegos, Isabel O., et al. "Bias and Fairness in Large Language Models: A Survey." *arXiv preprint*, arXiv:2309.00770, 2024, arxiv.org/pdf/2309.00770.

Gillespie, Tarleton. "The Relevance of Algorithms." *Media Technologies: Essays on Communication, Materiality, and Society*, edited by Tarleton Gillespie, Pablo J. Boczkowski, and Kirsten A. Foot, MIT Press, 2014, pp. 167–94.

Goffman, Erving. *Frame Analysis: An Essay on the Organization of Experience.* Harper & Row, 1974.

Goffman, Erving. *The Presentation of Self in Everyday Life.* Doubleday, 1959.

Goffman, Erving. *Stigma: Notes on the Management of Spoiled Identity.* Prentice-Hall, 1963.

Green, Melanie C. "Transportation into Narrative Worlds." *Entertainment-Education Behind the Scenes: Case Studies for Theory and Practice*, edited by Lauren B. Frank and Paul Falzone, Palgrave Macmillan, 2021, pp. 87–101.

Green, Melanie C., and Timothy C. Brock. "The Role of Transportation in the Persuasiveness of Public Narratives." *Journal of Personality and Social Psychology*, vol. 79, no. 5, 2000, pp. 701–721.

Grunig, James E., editor. *Excellence in Public Relations and Communication Management.* Lawrence Erlbaum Associates, 1992.

Grunig, James E., and Todd Hunt. *Managing Public Relations.* Holt, Rinehart and Winston, 1984.

Hall, Stuart. "Encoding/Decoding." *Culture, Media, Language: Working Papers in Cultural Studies, 1972–79*, edited by Stuart Hall et al., Hutchinson, 1980, pp. 128–138.

Hall, Stuart. "The Question of Cultural Identity." *Modernity and Its Futures*, edited by Stuart Hall, David Held, and Tony McGrew, Polity Press/Open University, 1992, pp. 273–316.

Hall, Stuart, Jessica Evans, and Sean Nixon. "Representation: cultural representations and signifying practices." (2024): 1-100.

Hobsbawm, Eric, and Terence Ranger, editors. *The Invention of Tradition*. Cambridge UP, 1983.

Hocking, Brian. "Rethinking the 'New' Public Diplomacy." *The New Public Diplomacy: Soft Power in International Relations*, edited by Jan Melissen, Palgrave Macmillan, 2005, pp. 28–43.

Ikenberry, G. John. Review of *Soft Power: The Means to Success in World Politics*, by Joseph S. Nye, Jr. *Foreign Affairs*, vol. 83, no. 3, May/June 2004, p. 136.

Jin, Dal Yong. "Korea's Cultural Diplomacy and the Political Economy of Soft Power." *Asian Perspective*, vol. 46, no. 1, 2022, pp. 93–117.

Johnson, Walter, and Francis J. Colligan. *The Fulbright Program: A History*. U of Chicago P, 1965.

Kaneva, Nadia. "Nation Branding: Toward an Agenda for Critical Research." *International Journal of Communication*, vol. 5, 2011, pp. 117–41.

Kavanagh, Jennifer, and Michael D. Rich. *Truth Decay: An Initial Exploration of the Diminishing Role of Facts and Analysis in American Public Life*. RAND Corporation, 2018, rand.org/pubs/research_reports/RR2314.html.

Kim, Youna. *The Soft Power of the Korean Wave: Parasite, BTS and Drama*. Routledge, 2021.

Kurbalija, Jovan. "The Evolving Significance of Soft Power: A Tribute to Joseph Nye." *Diplo*, 29 May 2025, diplomacy.edu/blog/evolving-significance-soft-power-tribute-joseph-nye/.

Lonergan, Erica D. "Disinformation, Deterrence and the Politics of Attribution." *International Affairs*, vol. 101, no. 3, 2025, pp. 967–985.

McClory, Jonathan. *The Soft Power 30: A Global Ranking of Soft Power*. Portland Communications, 2015.

McClory, Jonathan, and Olivia Harvey. "The Soft Power 30: Getting to Grips with the Measurement Challenge." *Global Affairs*, vol. 2, no. 3, 2016, pp. 309–19.

McCombs, Maxwell E., and Donald L. Shaw. "The Agenda-Setting Function of Mass Media." *Public Opinion Quarterly*, vol. 36, no. 2, 1972, pp. 176–187.

Melissen, Jan, editor. *The New Public Diplomacy: Soft Power in International Relations*. Palgrave Macmillan, 2005.

Miskimmon, Alister, Ben O'Loughlin, and Laura Roselle, editors. *Forging the World: Strategic Narratives and International Relations*. University of Michigan Press, 2017.

Miskimmon, Alister, Ben O'Loughlin, and Laura Roselle. *Strategic Narratives: Communication Power and the New World Order*. Routledge, 2013.

Muvunyi, Faustin, Giovanni-Maria Messina, and Innocent Ndayishimiye. "Cultural Heritage-Driven Nation Branding and Sustainable Development: Rebuilding National Identity in Rwanda." *African Journal of Empirical Research*, vol. 7, no. 1, 2026, pp. 1159–1173, doi.org/10.51867/ajernet.7.1.98.

Navigli, Roberto, et al. "Biases in Large Language Models: Origins, Inventory, and Discussion." *Journal of Data and Information Quality*, vol. 15, no. 2, 2023, article 10, doi.org/10.1145/3597307.

Nossel, Suzanne. "Smart Power." *Foreign Affairs*, vol. 83, no. 2, March/April 2004, pp. 131–42.

Nye, Joseph S., Jr. *Bound to Lead: The Changing Nature of American Power*. Basic Books, 1990.

Nye, Joseph S., Jr.. "Public Diplomacy and Soft Power." *The ANNALS of the American Academy of Political and Social Science*, vol. 616, no. 1, 2008, pp. 94–109.

Nye, Joseph S., Jr.. *The Paradox of American Power: Why the World's Only Superpower Can't Go It Alone*. Oxford UP, 2002.

Nyhan, Brendan. "Why the Backfire Effect Does Not Explain the Durability of Political Misperceptions." *Proceedings of the National Academy of Sciences*, vol. 118, no. 15, 13 April 2021, e1912440117, doi.org/10.1073/pnas.1912440117.

Park, Bernadette, and Myron Rothbart. "Perception of Out-Group Homogeneity and Levels of Social Categorization: Memory for the Subordinate Attributes of In-Group and Out-Group Members." *Journal of Personality and Social Psychology*, vol. 42, no. 6, 1982, pp. 1051–1068.

Pei, Gan, et al. "The Tug-of-War Between Deepfake Generation and Detection." *arXiv preprint*, arXiv:2407.06174, 2024, arxiv.org/html/2407.06174v4.

Rawnsley, Gary D. "To Know Us Is to Love Us: Public Diplomacy and International Broadcasting in Contemporary Russia and China." *Politics*, vol. 35, nos. 3–4, 2015, pp. 273–86.

Rogers, Richard, and Nicola Righetti. "Coordinated Inauthentic Behaviour on Facebook? A Typology of Manufactured Attention." *Social Media + Society*, 2025, doi.org/10.1177/29768624251369784.

Roselle, Laura, Alister Miskimmon, and Ben O'loughlin. "Strategic narrative: A new means to understand soft power." *Media, war & conflict* 7.1 (2014): 70-84.

Schiff, Kaylyn Jackson, Daniel S. Schiff, and Natália S. Bueno. "The Liar's Dividend: Can Politicians Claim Misinformation to Evade Accountability?" *American Political Science Review*, vol. 119, no. 1, 2025, pp. 71–90.

Schooler, Robert D. "Product Bias in the Central American Common Market." *Journal of Marketing Research*, vol. 2, no. 4, 1965, pp. 394–97.

Simon, Herbert A. "Designing Organizations for an Information-Rich World." *Computers, Communications, and the Public Interest*, edited by Martin Greenberger, Johns Hopkins UP, 1971, pp. 38–72.

Stougaard-Nielsen, Jakob. "Nordic Crime Fiction." *Nordics.info*, Aarhus University, nordics.info/show/artikel/crime-fiction. Accessed 23 April 2026.

Tajfel, Henri, and John C. Turner. "An Integrative Theory of Intergroup Conflict." *The Social Psychology of Intergroup Relations*, edited by W. G. Austin and S. Worchel, Brooks/Cole, 1979, pp. 33–47.

Taylor, Philip M. "Cultural Diplomacy and the British Council: 1934–1939." *British Journal of International Studies*, vol. 4, no. 3, 1978, pp. 244–65.

Trevor-Roper, Hugh. "The Invention of Tradition: The Highland Tradition of Scotland." *The

Invention of Tradition, edited by Eric Hobsbawm and Terence Ranger, Cambridge UP, 1983, pp. 15–41.

United States, Government Accountability Office. *China: With Nearly All U.S. Confucius Institutes Closed, Some Schools Sought Alternative Chinese Funding*. GAO-24-105981, Oct. 2023.

Verlegh, Peeter W. J., and Jan-Benedict E. M. Steenkamp. "A Review and Meta-Analysis of Country-of-Origin Research." *Journal of Economic Psychology*, vol. 20, no. 5, 1999, pp. 521–546.

Walker, Christopher, and Jessica Ludwig. *Sharp Power: Rising Authoritarian Influence*. National Endowment for Democracy, December 2017.

Walker, Christopher, and Jessica Ludwig. "The meaning of sharp power: How authoritarian states project influence." *Foreign affairs* 16.11 (2017).

Waltz, Kenneth N. *Theory of International Politics*. Addison-Wesley, 1979.

Zorthian, Julia. "Large Language Models Are Biased – Local Initiatives Are Fighting for Change." *Nature*, 28 Nov. 2025, nature.com/articles/d41586-025-03891-y.

ACKNOWLEDGMENTS

The acknowledgements that follow are set within the framework of nearly fifteen years devoted to international promotional activity – a long and intense season of work that carried me across three continents in service of Italian, and most especially Sicilian, excellence. Those years, spent building bridges between producers and markets, between cultural heritage and contemporary enterprise, form the backdrop against which the following expressions of gratitude must be read.

A heartfelt and deeply respectful thank you goes to The Hon. Dr. Francesco Giacobbe, whose friendship and esteem I regard as a true honour. His generous contribution of the preface to this volume is a gesture I receive with sincere gratitude and profound appreciation, and it lends these pages a value for which I shall always be indebted to him.

A very special thanks goes to Salvo Bonanno, with whom I worked shoulder to shoulder for ten years at the Italian Quality Handicrafts Consortium, and alongside whom I had the privilege of serving on the Board of the Italian American Chamber of Commerce of the Midwest. That remarkable chapter, which came to a close in 2015 – coinciding with the first edition of this book – left deep and lasting traces. In particular, a decade spent organising the presence of the Government of Sicily, my native region, at major international trade fairs proved to be an extraordinarily fulfilling endeavour, offering the opportunity to promote Sicilian craftsmanship across the world through the work of its very finest master artisans.

My heartfelt gratitude extends to the many outstanding professionals in the field of public relations who accompanied this journey – foremost among them Tom Madden, a distinguished name in American public rela-

tions, for whom I had the honour of working at the Florida-based Trans-media Group PR agency. I am equally indebted to the dedicated teams at the Chambers of Commerce, the Italian Trade Commissions, the Italian Cultural Institutes, and the many associations of Italians abroad – in particular the Order Sons and Daughters of Italy in America (OSDIA) and the National Italian American Foundation (NIAF) – as well as the Italian Embassies and Consulates, and Casa Sicilia, across the three continents touched by our promotional events.

To all of them, and to the countless friends and collaborators met along the way throughout these fifteen years of international engagement, my sincere and enduring thanks.

Carmelo Cutuli

In memory of Franco Cappelli

To Franco Cappelli, esteemed colleague and friend of ten years, who taught me that true professionalism rests on foundations at once simple and powerful – integrity, precision, and quiet dedication to the work. A consummate professional, an intrepid and adventurous traveller, he brought to every undertaking the same curiosity and courage with which he embraced the world.
This work is dedicated to his memory, in gratitude for the lessons shared, the journeys taken in thought and word, and the enduring example of a truly great man.

www.ingramcontent.com/pod-product-compliance
Lightning Source LLC
Chambersburg PA
CBHW071506220526
45472CB00003B/938